RUGBY REBEL

Rugby Rebel

The Alan Tait Story

ALAN TAIT WITH BILL LOTHIAN

MAINSTREAM
PUBLISHING

EDINBURGH AND LONDON

First published in Great Britain in 1998 by
MAINSTREAM PUBLISHING COMPANY (EDINBURGH) LTD
7 Albany Street
Edinburgh EH1 3UG

ISBN 1 84018 064 1

A catalogue record for this book is available from the British Library

Typeset in Garamond
Printed and bound in Great Britain by Butler and Tanner Ltd, Frome

Contents

Foreword by Bill McLaren   7

Foreword by Ray French   9

Preface   11

1   Pride . . . and Prejudice?   13
The journey back from rugby league

2   Charlie's Darlin'   28
Cumbria was my launch-pad

3   Poynder Pointers   39
Early lessons at Kelso Rugby Union Club

4   The Widnes Years   53
How I slotted into the dream team

5   Headingley Heaven and Hell   75
From the highs of Wembley to being shown the door

6   Tait on the Tyne   96
Revitalised by the epoch-breaking Newcastle Falcons

7   Foxes and Lions   115
Selection bias and a snub to Downing Street

8   Worlds Apart   135
Who's afraid of the All Blacks? Well, actually . . .

9   Bonnie and Clyde   151
     *Linford's narrow escape, plus how to use the
        off-season wisely*

10   A League of Nations?   161
     Putting Scottish rugby union to rights

11   So, Where Now?   179
     Fanfare to the common code

     Alan Tait's Career Record   185
     Statistics and data galore

Foreword by Bill McLaren

*Ex-Hawick and former Scotland trialist
BBC rugby union commentator*

It seemed in every sense appropriate that Alan Tait should receive the 1998 Famous Grouse Scotland Player of the Five Nations Championship award because his contribution to Scotland's international fortunes, both on and off the field, since his return from the rugby league game has been distinctive and influential, not only in the hard-nosed, mentally tough approach that so benefited Scotland's back play, especially in defence discipline, but also in the advisory influence he exerted on national-team colleagues.

It also seems appropriate that he and Bill Lothian should put on record a fascinating personal tale that traces his early days in Kelso and Workington to and beyond his rating as the first former rugby league player to be capped by Scotland.

It is a fascinating story that embraces his experience as a Kelso three-quarter who played for the South of Scotland fourteen times and scored six tries, also gaining eight caps in 1987 and 1988 before spending nine years with Widnes and Leeds in rugby league. He played fourteen times for Great Britain prior to his return to union with Newcastle Falcons, going on to gain a further eight Scotland caps as well as selection for the 1997 British Isles touring squad in South Africa.

This is a story in the style that Alan displays on the rugby field – forthright, honest and without frills. It captures the mixed fortunes and emotions of five playing visits to the famous Wembley Stadium as well as his reaction to the considerable challenge of returning to the union game, in which regard it was testimony to his character that there was no resentment at his speedy elevation to Scotland A and further cap status. It is a tale too about some outstanding try-scoring, nine in sixteen cap internationals and a Lions Test try in South Africa, most of them achieved with sundry opponents either clinging to him or having been bounced aside by power and dogged determination as well as intuitive running angles.

Alan Tait has been a credit to himself and to both codes in terms of attitude and commitment. His is a story worth telling and equally worth reading. And it may not yet be finished. He would give his all to play for Scotland in the 1999 World Cup, and who would wager against him doing so, even at the ripe old age of 35? He has never given less than his all throughout an illustrious career that now, in the telling, becomes a fascinating segment of the literature of the rugby game.

Bill McLaren, 1998

Foreword by Ray French

Ex-St Helens, Lancashire, Barbarians and England rugby union
Ex-St Helens, Widnes, Lancashire and Great Britain rugby league
BBC radio/television commentator

An appearance in a Challenge Cup final at Wembley or the donning of a Great Britain jersey for the first time can often have an unnerving effect on even the hardest of league players. But only those who, like myself, crossed the once-great divide between rugby union and rugby league can appreciate the nerves experienced by a former 15-a-side international as he waits to take the field before an often highly critical audience in the 13-a-side code.

Whatever a player's skills, speed, mental toughness or attitude in union, he stands a naked man on the touchlines of rugby league. He must first prove himself to his team-mates and then, by virtue of his ability, win over the fans on the terraces. Alan Tait did just that. From the moment the former Kelso centre arrived on the pitch at Naughton Park, Widnes, for a match against Halifax on 24 April 1988, to the day of his return to the union fold and Newcastle Falcons, he displayed the attributes and, above all, the determination to succeed in rugby league.

A Great Britain international within 12 months of his arrival in league, Alan not only carved out a glorious career for himself with Widnes and Leeds but, whether at home or in Papua New Guinea, France or New Zealand, also became the perfect ambassador for the code, both on and off the field. And, when sitting alongside him on a plane crossing the Tasman Sea, chatting to him at an after-match function or discussing pre-match tactics in a hotel lobby, one could not fail to appreciate his deep knowledge of, and respect for, rugby of both codes.

Unlike the Welsh, who have trekked north in their thousands over the past 100 years to find fame and fortune in rugby league, the number of Scottish players arriving in towns like Widnes, Wigan, Leeds and Huddersfield, especially in recent years, has been considerably less. Alan Tait became only the fourth player – joining Heriot's FP's Roy Kinnear, Jed-Forest's David Rose and Hawick's Dave Valentine – to play for Scotland at union and Great Britain at league. He is unique in that he has since returned across the border to add to his number of Scottish rugby union caps.

He has conducted himself with dignity in both codes of rugby and holds a special place in the hearts of all rugby followers, whatever their persuasion.

Thanks for the memories, Alan. I'll cherish those days spent in Garoka, Port Moresby, Auckland, Perpignan and, especially, at Naughton Park and Headingley for many years to come. As I'm sure you will.

Ray French, 1998

Preface

It's a long way from Murrayfield Stadium in Edinburgh to Naughton Park, home of Widnes Rugby League Club, or Headingley, where Leeds Rugby League Club play. But it is an even longer way back. So long, in fact, that nobody had ever made the return journey until I came along on 1 March 1997 to carve a little niche in what the commentators insisted was Scottish rugby history.

For over 100 years rugby league and rugby union had been at loggerheads. And then, in August 1995, the barriers came down, as it became increasingly and blindingly obvious that the professionalism which originally cut league adrift was rife in the mother code. The position of the so-called amateur authorities became unsustainable and so a free gangway opened up.

It was my good fortune to be in the right place at the right time to benefit from the epoch-breaking changes, which is why I am about to break the first rule of the paid ranks – namely that true professionals only look forward; it is the amateurs who look back!

So many people have helped me in the course of my rugby career(s) that I wish to attempt to put on record the reasons why I owe them so much, while also looking to predict the future for a great game going through a dramatic and prolonged change process.

In particular I should maybe pay tribute to my former Kelso and Scotland colleague John Jeffrey, bearing in mind my last game for Scotland in my original rugby union career coincided with that infamous 1988 match which saw him and England forward Dean Richards suffer varying degrees of punishment for damaging the Calcutta Cup during some wild revelry on the streets of Edinburgh. Knowing, as I'm sure he did, that I was set to sign rugby league forms a few days later, I've often marvelled at how John didn't succumb to the temptation to blame me for the dents in the silverware since I would soon be out of the jurisdiction of the rugby union authorities! And John Jeffrey was supposed to be one of the brighter members of the Kelso team I had the privilege of playing in . . .

On the other hand, of course, if I had taken the rap for John and left unpunished I suppose it is fair to assume there would have been no 'second coming' in a Scotland jersey, and I probably wouldn't be writing this!

Alan Tait
Stitchill, near Kelso

CHAPTER ONE

Pride . . . and Prejudice?

I don't know if I was more frightened of the Irish opposition or Caroline, my wife, as I lined up facing Murrayfield's magnificent west grandstand on 1 March 1997, awaiting our 'anthem'.

'Cry at "Flower of Scotland" and I'll give you a clout round the ear when you get home,' Caroline, not normally an aggressive person, had warned when I set off *en route* to an international rugby union comeback after eight years away playing rugby league.

I'm not noted for disobeying the commands of her indoors, but, I tell you, that was one occasion which might have proved an exception to the rule. To get one rugby cap for Scotland is special. To be granted two separate international careers after a spell among the hitherto untouchables of the professional code was an honour granted to no other rugby player. It was an emotional business out there on the pitch, while constantly aware of the attention of the television cameras. Make no mistake.

After just managing to keep the taps turned off, tackling the Irish was, with due respect, the easy bit. Or relatively so. But how on earth did I, Alan Victor Tait, find myself astride the Murrayfield turf, chest pushed out and hands tightly clasped behind my back, singing with such great gusto? Only a few years earlier the only way I'd have been invited to line up like that at Murrayfield would have been as target practice for a firing squad!

In the spring of 1995, the Scottish Rugby Union had, after all, issued the following message, clearly and unequivocally, in their international programme for the visit of Wales (you know, the match where Eric Peters scored that great try after lead-up work by Doddie Weir and Kenny Logan). Under the headline 'AMATEURISM', printed in big, black letters, obviously for extra emphasis, an editorial commissioned by the general committee eventually reached the following conclusion: 'It would seem that other than a very few, most people, including the players, want the game to remain amateur.'

Now, two years and three days later, the same Murrayfield programme was proclaiming the return of myself, a dyed-in-the-wool professional latterly of Widnes and Leeds rugby league clubs, to the Scottish international ranks for a match against Ireland.

Quite a turnaround – and one of the biggest conversions in Murrayfield history? What, in fact, had happened was that less than six months after the SRU committee's denunciation of professional rugby, the game's International Board, meeting in Paris, had decided that enough was enough and that it was time to stop living the lie and put an end to the shamateurism everybody knew was rife.

I wasn't bothered either by the politics of the game or the hypocrisy and double standards that had gone before. Just so long as I could help Scotland to victory. But I was aware, nonetheless, of the pressure stemming from having to uphold the honour of rugby league and the standards it set. If I flopped – and I suspected there were a few rugby union diehards hoping I would – then rugby league's image would take a battering also. That would be unacceptable, because to me they will *both* always be great games.

Pride comes before a fall, they say. If that's true, then when that comeback match was over and we'd beaten our Celtic cousins 38–10, I could have done with strapping a parachute to my back just for a bit of extra protection. Or maybe that should be cockiness rather than pride? There at the end of the players' tunnel at full-time stood Arthur Hastie, a beaming Scotland team manager. How did I, the prodigal returned, greet him? 'Well, Arthur,' I yelled, while surfing that wave of adrenalin known only to those who have experienced the highs of international sport, 'the things I have to do to pull your lot out of the shit.'

Arthur Hastie rolled his eyes and reeled backwards to convey amazement at my reaction to what was, nevertheless, Scotland's first win in seven starts. However, in searching too long for a suitable riposte to a jest he maybe felt contained a grain of truth, Hastie left himself open to a quick verbal follow-up: 'And you can quote me on that if you like . . .' I hollered back up the tunnel.

I think I may have been in the showers by the time Arthur gathered himself and registered disapproval to John Beattie, the former international who was working as a radio summariser and who was on hand to hoover up post-match quotes.

'Here, John. Did you hear what Taity, the cheeky git, just said to me?' volunteered Arthur.

John hadn't. Which meant the grateful newshound was all the more delighted to bounce the *bon mot* off the airwaves and straight into the *Herald* rugby diary he diligently compiles each week.

Oliver Twist, brass-necked though he was, especially when it came to second helpings, would probably have blanched at giving off such cheek. Me? I was tripping the light fantastic and without a care in the world in the first flush of victory. Looking back, it was outrageous even to joke that the win which helped put Scotland's rugby team temporarily back on the rails was down to me. Och, but what the hell. I had a lot to be chuffed about and it was maybe no bad thing I had unloaded some of the tension that had been building up inside from ten days earlier when the team announcement had been made. I just hadn't been sure to what extent my return had been welcomed by officialdom, and poor Arthur, a long-time family friend from the same home town of Kelso, copped the brunt of that uncertainty. What mattered most, however, was that I had shown, at the age of 32, that I could absorb the pressure of expectation both from outside the squad and from within. Especially within.

Step forward and take a bow, Kenneth McKerrow Logan.

Did I say Kenny Logan? At times I wondered if Scotland had selected on the wing for my comeback match Kenny's namesake Jimmy Logan, the renowned music-hall comedian.

Now, they reckon players should be willing to die for their team-mates, and after a few hours in Kenny's company before that Irish game this was something I appreciated better than ever. Except that I envisaged myself swinging on the end of a rope if I had executed what I contemplated doing to Kenny in return for being the main butt of his laugh-a-minute routine.

Much of Kenny's patter at my expense had centred on mimicking Eddie Waring. The late rugby league commentator wasn't everybody's cup of tea. It was felt in some quarters that he trivialised a great game he actually helped foster, both behind a microphone and as manager of a Dewsbury team who were virtually unbeatable during the Second World War. The argument went that by portraying himself as a typical cloth-cap northerner, Eddie, who was actually Australian, did much to restrict rugby league's attempts to expand beyond its original boundaries. Also, Eddie's ee-bah-gum Yorkshire accent was ripe for lampooning, a point seized on by Logan.

'Eers Alan Tait froom roogby leeague,' bellowed Kenny as the Scotland team mustered early in the week. 'Ee oop lad. Ee's a straight rooner is yon Tait.'

That, to Kenny, was the image of rugby league, and I don't blame him for that. But it was the image I was keen to dispel and see replaced with greater awareness that to play rugby league professionally as a back you have to be able to handle like a card-sharp, tackle like the clap of doom and run like the wind. League is anything but an easy option to get a few quid in the bank in return for leaving home for a few years.

I doubt whether Kenny was actually old enough to have heard Eddie Waring in full flow. It's a matter of record that Kenny wasn't born when Lawrie London had a hit in 1957 with a song entitled 'He's Got the Whole World in his Hands'. But that didn't stop the Stirlingshire farmer, destined soon after to join the English First Division club Wasps, from adding to my unease. 'He's Got the Whole World in his Hands' is a catchy number – and so easily adapted to 'He's Got the Whole World on his Shoulders'. And adapt that song is exactly what Kenny did.

As public intrigue at the notion of a former rugby league pro returning to the traditionally true-blue amateur world of Scottish rugby union grew, so that song became my personal theme tune. Regular renditions might have been a joke to Kenny and some of my fellow players. But you have no idea how close to the truth the words felt. I could hear that damn song reverberating in my skull as I lay awake at night in the big-match build-up. And it would still be there, dammit, first thing in the morning. How would I cope?

I began by convincing myself that if I could contribute to the preliminaries – a bit of chat, a training idea, maybe – that would be something, at least. Rob Wainwright, the Scotland skipper and a really switched-on guy, was especially good to me, with a bedside manner befitting the qualified doctor that he is. You might say Rob was different class in every sense, but I liked him from the start.

For someone from a totally different background and culture from me – he represented Glenalmond public school, Cambridge University and the Army, whereas I was a product of Moor Close Secondary in Workington before moving to Kelso High, which I left at the earliest possible opportunity aged 15 – we hit it off astonishingly well.

On the other hand, maybe our love of the countryside makes Rob and me similar in many ways. What with me and my love of hunting rabbits and ferreting with trained dogs and Rob's passion for falconry – rumour has it he once had a pet bird called Kevin which he tied to a brick in his living-room, allegedly to make it grow stronger – we got on like a house on fire.

I was really grateful to Rob for reminding the press that I wasn't the Messiah (his words not mine) during the countdown to the Irish game when it seemed I might be overwhelmed by a feeling of expectancy. Sure, I was flattered by the attention and the confidence of so many people that I could turn things around for Scotland, which I badly wanted to do. And I knew from the old days that playing rugby league was like playing international rugby union every week, probably harder. But I was certainly anxious that any suggestion that one player could galvanise a team should be nipped in the bud.

That's why I'd lie in bed at night frightened almost to death, and it hardly helped that I have always considered myself to be someone who really thinks a lot about my rugby. From the last training session on the Thursday evening to the final whistle on the Saturday or Sunday, it is total rugby all weekend so far as I'm concerned. I don't usually sleep much in the lead-up to a game, either, for thinking about the guy I'm going to be playing against, team tactics and what I'm going to be doing with the ball when it comes my way.

I'm a big believer in mental preparation and, for example, I hate finishing on a bad training session. In rugby league everything had to be spot on, and the last 20 minutes of training before a match were always short and sharp with the emphasis on pinpoint accuracy. The way I got through that Irish match build-up was by reminding myself constantly that once the game started it was only the number 13 for Ireland, Maurice Field, a fireman from the Malone club in Ulster, that I really had to bother about. If I dampened down Maurice's personal fire, I'd be doing my job. That's the attitude I eventually took with me into the Scotland dressing-room.

As the week of the Irish match wore on, I started to forget any supposed burden of expectation and relaxed a bit. But gnawing at the back of my mind was how I'd react to singing 'Flower of Scotland'. When I had previously played for Scotland the Scottish Rugby Union hadn't sanctioned the anthem. As far as I'm aware, it was Finlay Calder who, during his term as national captain in 1989, took the idea to the SRU committee on behalf of the players with a view to having the song adopted as an equivalent to 'Land of my Fathers', which was always such an inspiration to the Welsh team, especially at Cardiff Arms Park. From the start, and with permission duly obtained from the lyricists, The Corries folk duo, the playing of 'Flower of Scotland' was an instant hit with players and crowd alike.

When I first heard 'Flower of Scotland' sung by the players I was in France on rugby league duty with Great Britain and was watching on television. It moved me from afar and I remember thinking, 'What a fantastic way to build yourself up for an international.' I loved it from the start, and my blood pumps whenever they play it. In fact, I couldn't believe it when, in early 1998, there was actually a debate in political circles over the need for another Scottish anthem. What nonsense. 'Flower of Scotland' is good enough for me and occupied my thoughts on and off during international week, and especially as kick-off neared.

In the dressing-room, I felt the emotion of the occasion over-powering me as Rob Wainwright began to deliver the final team talk, and tears were welling in my eyes. So much so that I started hitting my chest and slapping my face to try to make my eyes water and cover the fact that this so-called hard-nosed pro was just a big softie at heart. I'm glad the dam burst in the privacy of that inner sanctum, enabling me to get the emotion out of my system, for reasons explained at the outset, but it was still no easy matter keeping my true feelings in check when entering the arena.

When referee Gareth Simmonds, from Wales, finally blew his whistle for the teams to line up for the kick-off, I began to think even more profound thoughts, centred on Scots who had gone to rugby league, none of whom had made it back to union. To mark my first rugby league cap a magazine had even printed a table of what they called 'ten Scots to excel in rugby league'. They were (in order): 1. Alan Tait, jnr; 2. Alan Tait, snr; 3. George Fairbairn; 4. Dave Valentine; 5. Brian Shillinglaw; 6. Alex Fiddes; 7. Ron Cowan; 8. Drew Broatch; 9. Harry Whitaker; 10. Alex Cassie.

I was able to add a few of my own, namely Hugh Duffy, David Rose, George 'Happy' Wilson and George Swanston, as well as Roy Kinnear, a Herioter who had moved to Wigan and who was father of the late comedian. Not a lot of people know that, I suspect! I'm sure they were all with me, the first man back from rugby league to play for Scotland, and as the band cleared the pitch I said a silent 'thank you' to the modern SRU for letting me have my chance.

After all the fuss and hullaballoo, trust me to be involved in a desperate start for Scotland, who fell seven points behind to a try from Irish winger Dennis Hickie, converted by David Humphreys. Fortunately things could only get better and, appropriately, some typical rugby league tactics played a huge part in our recovery.

A favourite saying in rugby league is 'hard yards'. It's the territorial advantage gained from driving at the opposition and stacking up all those inches gained by struggling forward in the tackle – *New Scientist* magazine even produced an article on the subject a couple of years ago. Best at putting in the 'hard yards' on my return against Ireland was undoubtedly Tom Smith, the prop who was to make a name for himself on the 1997 British Lions tour of South Africa. Wild and windy conditions dictated that Scotland kept the ball close to the forwards, and that approach was right up Tom's street.

It also suited me to play a backing-up game similar to rugby league, which is how I came to be in position to take a pass from Craig Chalmers and claim the try which levelled the scores just before half-time. A couple of months later that score was to be voted 'try of the season' by viewers of BBC's *Sportscene Rugby Special* and earn me a cool £1,000 from competition sponsors Highland Spring, but, I have to confess, the try hardly had much in the way of aesthetic quality. Pretty it was not, unless you like rapid recycling of possession from mini-rucks, although I suppose my angle of running at the point of breakthrough was pretty decent.

The second half saw us smother Ireland with our close-quarter control and I resisted any temptation to go for the line myself, sending winger Tony Stanger in for our final try in a 38–10 win.

To get that Irish game successfully out of the way was a massive relief. With pressure, though, comes pride in equal measure once the job is completed satisfactorily, and at full-time thoughts were for my wife, Caroline, and parents, Alan and Maureen.

I've always been a believer that if things are right at home then the rest of your life is more likely to fall into place. It was later, once I got back to the bungalow in the Borders village of Stitchill, near Kelso, that my Dad, a joiner, built with the money I got from rugby league, that I began thinking more about the implications of my achievement for Michael and Zoey, my children. They might one day tell their kids, my grandchildren, that I had come back from rugby league and not only resumed playing international rugby union but scored a try into the bargain!

The reviews made good reading. While the Irish coach Brian Ashton felt his side should have used their early whip-hand as a springboard to victory, Scottish critics appeared convinced the home team had taken a notable step forward. Derek Bateman described my comeback by telling *Scotland on Sunday* readers,

> Tait marked his return after eight years in the other code with a try, taking Craig Chalmers' pass from an inside break and taking two tacklers over the line with him. What he brought to the Scotland plan was organisation, nous and mental focus that comes from playing for a living for so long.
>
> Absolute concentration is so often lacking in Scotland's game. It's why kick-offs and restarts are surrendered weakly and why panic sets in with the try-line open. Chances were spurned as usual yesterday, the inability to give or take a crucial pass letting the Scots down.
>
> Yet Tait was not guilty of such sin. Tait began with a classic tackle on stand-off David Humphreys, had an unsuccessful sally into two Irishmen on the crash ball and couldn't be faulted on the Irish try.
>
> Tait bristled with determination. Although he could never live up completely to unrealistic expectations, he couldn't resist calling the shots to colleagues and encouraging all around him.

He appeared as auxiliary full-back and kept his position under pressure instead of being pulled away during Irish attacks. These are as much the attributes of the men who wear the number 15 jersey as they are of those with the number 13, and thoughts ran to placing the Kelso man at full-back when Rowen Shepherd began so lamely. Shepherd grew into a big game, yet the thought remains that full-back might be the ultimate position for Tait's skills.

Tait was the vital link, witness his pass to Tony Stanger, who dropped it with all the options open to him. Tait has replaced Scott Hastings but, on paper, you'd wonder what the difference was between the two hard-running, tough-tackling players. The money may not be so good as it is in league, but you can bet Tait won't regret his return to union.

From the perspective of the British press, Bill Day had this to say in the *Mail on Sunday*:

Alan Tait relaunched his international career with the try that sent Scotland racing to victory by a record margin over the Irish.

Nine years after he last wore the blue jersey, the Newcastle centre plunged between the Irish ranks to score the first of five tries and end Scotland's fears of a Five Nations whitewash. The relief of the Scots was almost tangible after their Twickenham drubbing and Murrayfield defeat by Wales, and the delight on Tait's face was as clear as on any occasion during his distinguished league career.

The watching Lions tour manager Fran Cotton must have been impressed with the flair that Tait's return brought to a rejuvenated side. Scotland coach David Johnston reckoned Tait's 'buoyancy and competence' had injected enthusiasm, and Ireland coach Brian Ashton conceded that Tait had made a major contribution to his team's defeat.

And from within the camp, colleague Tony Stanger repaid me for the scoring pass by stating, 'Alan's enthusiasm is brilliant – and it's rubbing off on the rest of us.'

I had made it back and confounded some who suspected old

prejudices would prevail (including a certain ex-SRU president, who apparently told golfing chums I'd be recalled over his dead body!) when I did not get instant promotion from the Scotland A team which thumped Emerging Wales at Goldenacre, Edinburgh, during January 1997. It was certainly an outstanding team performance to finish on the comfortable end of a 56–11 scoreline. And, to be honest, I knew very little in advance about the Scotland A team, since I had only returned to rugby union with Newcastle Falcons a few months earlier. When I moved to Widnes from Kelso in 1988, Andy Nicol was beginning a record three successive seasons in the Scottish Schools side at scrum-half, and as for the other full internationals selected – Peter Wright, Carl Hogg, Eric Peters and Stewart Campbell – I'd only seen them play on television. On the other hand, the Emerging Wales team had a familiar look, and in Leigh Davies they had a centre whom I had rated outstanding in the previous year's Five Nations Championship.

Man of the match, though, turned out to be the young Scottish winger James Craig who, in racing clear for three of our seven tries, had a sufficient turn of pace to remind me of Martin Offiah, the Great Britain rugby league winger alongside whom I had played so often for Widnes.

'Rumour has it that James has run 10.8 seconds for 100 metres mucking about,' I noted afterwards, adding, 'That was what Martin was timed at wearing running spikes by the GB rugby league coaches.' I went on to say, 'James is a frighteningly good prospect for Scotland, especially as he has done what he has without really concentrating on developing his physique.' If James, son of a former Celtic footballer who starred in the 1967 European Cup-winning team, ever needs an agent, he knows where to contact me!

It was a measure of Scotland A's dominance that some of the Welsh fans in an 8,000 crowd booed their side off the field, and I played my part in their discomfort with a break which sent James Craig over to complete his hat-trick.

The critics were especially kind to the entire team, as you'd expect in such circumstances, and Stuart Bathgate, writing in *The Scotsman*, said, 'Tait's marshalling of his defence was just as acutely intelligent as his angles of attack.'

The die had, then, been cast in the event of Scotland failing to produce the goods the following day against Wales, and when that duly happened – hopes falling apart in a second-half salvo of tries – I was widely tipped for a step up. To reinforce their demands, most pundits were noting the contribution made to the senior Welsh cause by ex-league centres Allan Bateman and Scott Gibbs as well as former Wigan loose forward Scott Quinnell and prop Dai Young, a past captain of Salford.

In fact, I had predicted in a pre-Five Nations Championship interview with Kevin Ferrie, then of *Scotland on Sunday*, that the ex-league pros would revitalise Wales. I told Kevin, 'Wales will now be a really good side, well drilled. These lads will have come into that dressing-room with a bang, and one thing their years in rugby league will have given them is discipline. However, what Wales will have more than anything is the confidence that has been missing. The league boys will have arrived with a smile on their faces and will lift the dressing-room morale, but underneath is that discipline of the training ground.'

I also predicted a brighter future for rugby union in general, remarking, 'I found it [rugby union] pretty hard to watch a few years ago, but it has changed dramatically and I went to Newcastle because I knew it was a club that was serious about its intentions, and they have a fitness programme that's right up there with the world's best.

'However, the more important thing is the change in attitude on the pitch. I got the shock of my life the first time I came to Newcastle and, if we were given a penalty anywhere near the line, Gary Armstrong just tapped and ran. It was so different from the days when everything would have stopped and we would have marched back and taken a kick at goal. I would be lying if I said that, as a back, union wasn't easier than league. But it is getting faster all the time.'

When the team to face England in Scotland's next fixture came out, my name was missing. But, amidst a fair old media furore, I had to agree with the Scotland coach, Richie Dixon, when he explained my absence, saying, 'Alan Tait has only played six games of rugby union and two first-class matches, including Scotland A versus Emerging Wales. Obviously this makes his performance against the Welsh all the more remarkable. Alan Tait is down for a further run in the A team – for his benefit and ours.'

I was maybe relieved to be missing the trip to Twickenham even though it was the only ground on the Five Nations circuit I had still to appear at, a situation which, incidentally, remained unchanged until the final match of the 1997–98 club season.

A lot of Newcastle's matches had been postponed during December and January because of bad weather, and there had been few opportunities to get much-needed match practice after so long in rugby league. The selectors were actually quite right in saying that I, a 'young 32', according to Scotland A boss Dougie Morgan, didn't have enough experience, ironic though that sounds.

Nevertheless, I knew within myself that years of daily weight training and generally looking after my diet were about to give me a keen edge in the world of professional rugby union, where, inevitably and to an extent understandably, mistakes were being made on a daily basis. I also knew that by the time selection for the Irish match – a more realistic target – came around I would have had the opportunity of another half-dozen quality club matches with Newcastle.

As fate would have it I missed the A international where Scotland went down 52–17 to England because of an infection in the groin area which, I was amazed to read, had become career-threatening. Nothing could have been further from the truth. I had a problem with a tooth which led to an infection, which in turn affected my leg. A course of antibiotics quickly did the trick, but by that stage the England A match had come and gone.

The forwards on duty for what turned out to be a record 41–13 defeat at Twickenham remained intact for the Irish encounter which followed a month later. But added to the backs were myself, Duncan Hodge and the uncapped Cammy Glasgow. Axed were Derek Stark, Ronnie Eriksson and Scott Hastings, an old adversary and colleague from as far back as the inaugural rugby union World Cup in 1987.

At the media conference to announce the squad for the Irish match, David Johnston was highly complimentary in stating my attributes, saying, 'Alan Tait seems to be firing on all cylinders right now. I saw him playing against Scott Hastings a few weeks ago and Scott came out second in comparison.' It was a seal of approval from David that was much appreciated, because I knew him to be his own man and determined not to be hustled into selecting me on the back of what he had called a bandwagon set rolling by the media.

It seemed to me that a sizeable number of Scottish Rugby Union people had been intent on keeping rugby league at arm's length, and it was reassuring to receive a further reminder that David, the ex-Watsonian centre with whom I had twice toured on Scotland's behalf many years previously, was from a different school. Indeed, David had given me a clear signal to 'hang in' as far as representative honours were concerned when I first appeared back on the rugby union scene, and he defended the right to reserve his position as a selector, saying, 'It doesn't help the profile of the game if any anti-rugby-league bias is promoted. Look, we have picked New Zealanders, South Africans, Germans and a hell of a lot of Englishmen [for Scotland, and all suitably qualified, of course]. We are hardly likely to ignore two Scots [George Graham, a prop-forward colleague at Newcastle, was also knocking at the door] who are definitely up there. It is just nonsense.'

Also, my comeback was, of course, uncomfortably close to the 'Meadowbank fiasco' of August 1995. On that occasion players due to represent Scotland in an amateur rugby league international against North-East England were warned in early-morning phone calls from Murrayfield that they risked being barred from rugby union for playing alongside professionals. One of those phoned was Boroughmuir scrum-half Andy Knight, who told the *Edinburgh Evening News* when the incident was highlighted in the week of my return to the international scene, 'When our team got together the league pros offered to stand down even though they were playing for nothing. But we stuck together as a team, convinced we had the law on our side, although a couple of players were so anxious they could hardly concentrate on the game.

'At first when I got the call I thought it was friends playing a joke on me. Then I realised it was serious. The commotion caused by the SRU's attitude to unpaid players representing Scotland at rugby league generated a lot of public support for us, and the SRU had to look at themselves and accept how silly their stance was becoming. I like to think we knocked a brick or two out of the wall which existed between the two codes.'

I have to say that some of the prejudices shown towards league were ridiculous in the extreme, and if my presence in the Scottish jersey symbolised the new 'open' game, all well and good. I was certainly keen to contribute to any feeling that rugby union had become a more honest sport. Gone were the days of brown envelopes carrying inflated expense claims being passed under the table, and the same went for those iffy and contrived schemes allowing players to be paid for appearing at events provided they were 'non-rugby related' – whatever that meant. For goodness sake, every sport needs to have heroes to give it as high a profile as possible.

I had, incidentally, caught my first whiff of the hypocrisy surrounding rugby union just prior to my Scotland début at that World Cup in New Zealand. Along with other members of the squad I had been struck by television advertisements featuring Andy Dalton, the All Black captain, riding across the screen on a tractor during commercial breaks. How come, we asked, Dalton is allowed to exploit his fame in such a way and obviously for reward at a time when no player is supposed to gain materially from rugby union either through playing or by association? 'Ah,' said the wiseacres on the ruling body. 'Andy Dalton is advertising tractors in his capacity as a farmer and not on account of his fame as the All Black captain.' Aye, sure. Pull the other leg!

Effectively it wasn't a tractor Dalton was driving. It was a horse and cart – right through the doomed amateur regulations. Still, the authorities proved unwilling to open their eyes to the fact that the rules were being exploited.

Nor would Scottish administrators budge from their view that in Scotland infringements were minimal when Kevin Campbell, a former Hawick forward playing in France and an ex-Scotland Under-21 colleague of mine, went on record in March 1995 to say that he received £200 a week from the French First Division club Mandelieu.

I really did dislike some of the hypocrisy attached to rugby union at one time, but if you think I am overreacting, please remember that few modern players have experienced, as I have, the slings and arrows, brickbats and put-downs, associated with crossing the rugby divide.

How it must have hurt my Dad, also a rugby league player, all those years ago on being asked to leave his old rugby union club-rooms when he returned one night for a drink. All because he had taken himself off to Northern England to ensure a better lifestyle for our family – Mum Maureen, younger sister Jacqueline and myself.

When I made my return to the Scotland team, I knew that Ronnie Cowan, who left Selkirk rugby union club as a British Lion in 1962 and joined Leeds rugby league club, was taking an interest in the comeback. Now a knitwear company representative back in the Borders, Ronnie had been asked by the press to sum up the significance of my return, and he responded in some style. Pulling no punches, he was reported by the *Edinburgh Evening News* as follows: 'The Scottish selectors must have had to swallow hard before picking Alan to face Ireland. Bringing in Tait is Scottish rugby's equivalent to the Berlin Wall coming down.' To compare my situation with the easing of repression in Eastern Europe was maybe stretching it a little bit. But see what I meant about pressure?

But to someone like Ronnie Cowan, shunned to the extent of being forced to coach a youth rugby union team in his home town by passing on instructions from over a hedge, my call-up had special poignancy symbolising real acceptance back into the fold. Ronnie, after all, maintains that the cruellest of many snubs delivered to him was being invited to travel to London as part of a business initiative along with other Borderers who had gained British Lions honours. However, the day after the invitation was issued Ronnie received a letter informing him that, as he had contravened amateur rugby union regulations, he was not welcome on the delegation. Suddenly it didn't appear to matter that his presence had initially been considered likely to boost the success of the mission. What price the local economy when there are decades-old prejudices to be reinforced?

Cowan is also on record as stating, 'When I returned to the Borders from 11 years in rugby league I was bursting with information I wanted to pass on. But I was chased from my local ground at Selkirk by order of the Scottish Rugby Union on so many occasions I eventually accepted that I couldn't go on embarrassing friends.' Where was the logic in banning a man with so much experience from contributing on a voluntary basis?

I firmly believe that rugby union missed out through attitudes shown towards Ronnie Cowan, my Dad and others. So, as well as trying to help Scotland defeat Ireland, I had to prove exactly what the 15-a-side code had denied itself.

CHAPTER TWO

Charlie's Darlin'

Goodness knows what persuaded Charlie Wright, then headmaster at my old school, Moor Close Secondary, Workington, to undertake a journey which landed him on the doorstep of the Tait family home for the first time one fine evening in the early 1980s. But I'll always be grateful to this large, avuncular sports fanatic for a visit that undoubtedly shaped my life for the better.

We'd just finished tea when my Dad answered the knock and found Charlie framed in the doorway. Charitable to a fault, Dad naturally assumed that only policemen came as big as Charlie and immediately suspected I had committed some minor misdemeanour. So, having braced himself for the worst, he was rather taken aback when Charlie introduced himself with the words, 'Good evening, Mr Tait. I'd just like to say this. I've put some rugby players through my hands, but your Alan is an exceptional prospect. Make sure you feed him well, because he'll play for his country one day. No doubt about it.'

It's Dad's recollection that Charlie was gone just as quickly as he had arrived. But the message certainly registered.

I've no doubt at all that it is every father's wish to give his offspring the opportunities which bypassed himself, and, for sure, Dad made a good enough living out of rugby league as well as acquiring a stack of lifelong friends. But the gaining of representative honours was aspired to by people other than Dad, a former three-quarter who turned out for Kelso and then played 134 games for Workington Town.

Charlie's visit got Dad thinking, and before long he had drawn up a plan based on a supposition that, as a Scot living in Cumbria, I had a less than average chance of realising any international potential I might or might not possess. After all, I had no English ancestry and the Scottish exiles' scouting system in rugby union, which eventually brought many fine players to the notice of the Murrayfield authorities, was very much in its infancy. On top of that, Cumbria really was a bit of a sporting backwater, much as I loved the place. My Mum was apparently told in no uncertain terms to prepare to return to the Borders, where I might be more easily spotted by a rugby talent scout.

Besides, at the age of 34 Dad knew his career in rugby league was swiftly coming to an end and it would soon be time to rely once again on his joinery skills for a living. Our family – my sister Jacqueline is three years younger than me – had moved to Workington 11 years earlier when Dad received an offer to leave Kelso for rugby league after being tapped by the legendary Jack 'Darcy' Anderson from Hawick. A former Scotland winger before going to rugby league, Darcy had been keeping an eye out for prospective converts, and as a result of information he passed on, Dad had the option of joining two or three clubs. Workington Town eventually won his signature for the princely sum of £6,000, but it was really a one-horse race in the end. My Mum's sister, Winnie, and her brother, Albert, lived in Workington, which meant there would be a familiar face or two there to look out for us should homesickness set in.

So, after a senior rugby union career which had started for Kelso against Jed-Forest – coincidentally as mine was to do – and included appearances at the prestigious Melrose Sevens, Dad threw his lot in with rugby league. Not that I knew too much about the upheaval. After all, I was only three and had to wait another six years before being introduced to rugby – by a woman.

I was always keen on sport and it was a famous day when I was allowed to start practising to play for the Victoria Primary School rugby league team. Alas, the teacher who was due to organise that first practice session was called away, so a colleague, Mrs Molly Nixon, stepped into the breach and remained in charge. Mrs Nixon made me captain and for the next two years our team travelled around Cumbria playing against opposition from Whitehaven, Barrow-in-Furness, Maryport and so on.

Those early days were important in instilling in me the basic skills of passing and tackling, and I remain firmly convinced that youngsters should have a grounding in rugby league before deciding whether or not to move on to rugby union. It's significant that some of the great Australian rugby union players such as Tim Horan and Jason Little started out this way. Rugby league is a much simpler game and the complexities of trying to stay upright at rucks are removed. There are fewer laws open to varying interpretations and the kids just have to concentrate on those twin basics of tackling and passing.

So I must admit my hackles were raised a year or two back when Jim Telfer, in his capacity as Scotland's director of rugby, took what I reckoned at the time to be a cheap shot at rugby league. Telfer was reported as saying, 'Our own game is far too cluttered and there will have to be law changes. But rugby league is such a simple game, any simpleton can watch it, and it can be very boring.'

Telfer's remarks followed an announcement by the New Zealand Rugby Union that they would be allowing rugby league players to return and pick up on the 15-a-side code without any proposed stand-down period. The point he was making was that rugby league was on borrowed time because the business world was more likely to focus on the more sophisticated of the two codes as the professional era bedded down. At the time I felt angry at such a denouncement of league, but I now understand it was not his intention to be dismissive. Rather he was just stressing that league was a more straightforward sport requiring, for better or for worse, less of an intellect to grasp – which is exactly why I would advocate rugby league for small children, who have enough to do handling and ensuring nobody gets past without burdening them with extra dimensions at too early an age.

Anyway, back at Victoria Primary School it was to Charlie Wright's further credit that dedication to duty persuaded him to fix up a meeting with Mrs Nixon at which he asked her to point out the best players in our side. This was all part of a cunning plan. I was mentioned by Mrs Nixon as having a modicum of talent, along with Ian Bower and John Hunter. After the summer holidays, when I entered Moor Close, I found we were in the same class as the pick of all the rugby players from the school's feeder primaries.

Charlie Wright had done his homework and provided me with a first glimpse into the art of team-building. As he put what he considered key players in the same class we all became best friends, which contributed enormously to the success of a team obliged, for reasons best known to the education authorities, to switch to rugby union at secondary school level. In fact by the time we were all 13 we were the best rugby union team in Cumbria, which justified my decision to give up football after aspiring to the giddy heights of a Cumbria Schools Under-13 trial as a right-back.

As a reward Charlie took us to play a school in Yorkshire, but when two of our key players, Glen Burgess and Neville Weaver, said they couldn't travel because their parents weren't able to afford the trip, I learned another valuable lesson at the hands of my mentor. Glen and Neville were our scrum-half and stand-off respectively and were vital to the team. Recognising this, Charlie sat them down and described them as the pedal and cog. I still remember his words, which were, 'Listen, lads. Without the pedal and the cog the bike won't go. The rest of the boys need you two along as well. See what you can do about persuading your folks.' Lifted by Charlie's persuasive rhetoric, they somehow found the means to make the 'tour'. The message Charlie was putting across, of course, was that we were all in it together, and this philosophy is one I've taken with me throughout my life in professional sport, along with an awareness of the debt sport owes to the teaching profession.

Charlie got his team away on a 'tour' which was subject to specific dos and don'ts. Strictly applied as well, they were. For a start, reveille was at 7 a.m., when we had to dip in a stream in the Yorkshire Dales. Everybody had to duck under the water for ten seconds because Charlie was an ex-Army type and believed it would be character-building. One morning we awoke to pelting rain and, to our delight, the stream was out of bounds. But there was no respite. Instead we had to have a cold bath – by order of Charlie. Such an experience at a tender age certainly didn't dampen my enthusiasm for rugby, however, while Glen Burgess went on to become an assistant coach at Workington Town after ten years as a player. Ian Bower, another member of that team, also embarked on a professional career. Actually, Glen still keeps in touch and occasionally encourages me to cast an eye over an up-and-coming Cumbrian youngster he thinks might make the grade.

If our headmaster at Moor Close was a forward-planner, his first lieutenant, Tom Borthwick, the PE master, was active in the field as captain of Aspatria rugby union club. And, fine teacher though Tom undoubtedly is, I'm sure those playing credentials alone would have been more than enough to have gained him the PE job at Moor Close School because Charlie Wright was proud of producing players for the Cumbria county team. Each one selected for representative duty brought further honour to the school, and Charlie once outlined part of his philosophy on education, saying, 'Kids who were not desperately academic still needed to feel important and wanted. One thing I reckoned we could do for them when I became head of the school in 1967 was to identify a form of excellence for these young-sters to pursue.

'Rugby was in my blood, but the main reason for choosing it as the school's principal sport was the fact that it was so much part of the local culture in Cumbria. Some members of staff thought I was a bit too keen on rugby – but we didn't half win a lot of cups!'

At primary school I had loved playing scrum-half because I had the ball in my hands all the time. When I went to Moor Close Tom Borthwick picked me at stand-off, inside centre and then outside centre. I could see myself getting further and further from the action and one day plucked up the courage to ask, 'Sir, why am I getting pushed out?' Tom replied, 'The further I get you away from the scrum the better, because once you get the ball nobody else gets it.'

Tom was right. Give me the ball at the end of a move and I'll score tries, as I hope I demonstrated satisfactorily on the wing for the British Lions and with Great Britain as a full-back in rugby league. Tom had pointed me in the right direction, aged 13, but I'll never be able to thank Charlie Wright enough for his prompting. It was reassuring to learn recently that Charlie is still going strong and living in his cottage on the main street in the Cumbria village of St Bees. That's when he can get through the door, past a remarkable collection of books, some of which sit underneath a portrait of one of his distant relatives, William Beilby! Apparently Beilby combined being a physician in Edinburgh with a calling as an evangelist. According to Charlie, some of his patients were less than enamoured when, on going for a medical consultation, they were asked if they were ready to meet their maker!

Charlie, though, really is a remarkable character whose cheerful, outgoing nature made him the ideal teacher. The son of a champion golfer and a qualified MCC cricket coach in his own right, Charlie still runs a mini-rugby team at Aspatria while keeping an eye on the sporting prowess of his grandson, Ben Chapman, a YTS soccer player at Grimsby Town.

Charlie didn't even become a rugby coach until the age of 40 and was an unlikely choice as head of a Workington local authority secondary school. A former pupil of Cheltenham College, which, it is claimed, is the oldest rugby-playing school in England after Rugby School, he read history at Oxford University. Somehow he found his way north after a spell living in Kenya, and it is testimony to his enthusiasm that he produced another international in England's David Pears.

Some of Charlie's coaching must have rubbed off on his own son, Edwin, who was good enough to spend a season or two in the crack Stade Toulouse side. Interestingly, Charlie tells of his son picking up an £80 match fee just for sitting on the Toulouse substitutes' bench in the days when, of course, rugby union was supposedly amateur!

Rarely, if ever, did I cross swords with Charlie, because of our mutual love of sport. This must have grated with a few of my pals, because on one occasion I was more or less dared to contrive a situation where I got the cane in the headmaster's office. As I recall, the conversation went something like this:

AT: 'I've been sent to see you, sir.'

Charlie: 'All right. Any more behaviour like that and you'll get the cane.'

AT: 'That's what you said last time, sir. And the time before that.'

Charlie could hardly refuse to give me four of the best, which were well worth receiving in order to prove I wasn't a teacher's pet. Which, of course, I suspect I was – along with every other member of Charlie's beloved rugby team.

Digging up roots and moving back to Kelso was very, very hard, not least because I had acquired a Cumbrian accent which I retain to this day. With that twang – somehow my sister slipped easily into Borders dialect – I expected trouble, even though I was 100 per cent Scottish.

On the credit side I'd had a far better grounding in rugby through my experience of both codes, which helped when I discovered that tackling at Kelso High often amounted to grabbing an opponent round the collar. At the very first training session I attended after moving to the Borders I inadvertently put on an exhibition of what would today be called 'big hits' and for a while got myself branded a little smart ass by my fellow pupils.

That wasn't how I envisaged breaking myself into new surroundings, but one day a big guy called Steven Hardcastle came charging through a ruck with knees pumping, scattering defenders to the wind, with the teacher, Bert Smith, screaming encouragement. Something had to be done, so I lined Steven up – and chopped him to the turf. The whistle went immediately and Bert gathered us round. I was braced for a telling-off as Steven lay on the ground, possibly even close to tears, never having been tackled properly in his life before. Instead Bert told the group, 'Did you see that? That's how to tackle. Let's continue and see if the rest of you can do the same.'

A few members of that team were destined to go on and make their mark at senior level. David 'Skrog' Shiel gained a Scotland B cap, while my namesake Alan 'Gel' Tait captained Melrose to a Division One title and has also enjoyed coaching success after being forced to retire from playing on account of a back injury. Chris 'Pussy' Bell has represented Melrose at top level while Gregor Walker was an accomplished winger with Kelso.

Following my crunching tackle I could see Steven Hardcastle giving me a big stare out of the corner of my eye. I was sure this would be the prelude to my first playground fight. In fact, we became friends, although I don't see Steven much now that he is a sergeant-major in the Army.

Steven and I started to go ferreting for rabbits along with another great mate, Kevin Armstrong, and his Dad, Jimmy, now sadly passed on. I still don't know if it was part of a long-term plan that my Dad left me to my own recreational devices. I'm sure he would have been disappointed if I hadn't realised the rugby potential he must have felt I had when he moved the family back from Cumbria. But he didn't push.

Whatever Dad's motives were, I enjoy seeing my own son, Mike, going off to mini-rugby, but I likewise don't watch him all that much. It's not that I'm not interested. Far from it. But at the back of my mind is the fact that my Dad was scared I wasn't going to go for it and that if he pushed too hard I would rebel against rugby. Or maybe he felt it was unfair to expect me to be good at rugby just because he had made a decent fist of it.

What I was aware of was that Dad always kept a trained eye on what I was doing rugby-wise. This I know because the pitch I played on as an Under-Nine in Cumbria lay adjacent to our terraced house situated in Frosthams Road, which was one of the best-known locations in Workington. There was nothing salubrious about Frosthams Road, but everybody knew where it was because the great Bill Shankly, sage of Liverpool Football Club, had stayed in the street during a spell in charge at Workington Reds FC early in his managerial career.

Anyway, Dad didn't venture out of the door to stand on the touchline but I could tell from the plumes of cigarette smoke going up in front of the window that he was keeping in touch with my progress. A pattern was set early, incidentally, because my Dad has been to Murrayfield only once to see me playing, and even that wasn't for the full Scotland side. Rather, he turned up at a B match against France (switched from Aberdeen) and to this day he complains that I never got a pass while he caught a cold sitting in the draughty grandstand. Despite that I know he is proud of my achievements. He has always been there for me, and he has kept my feet firmly on the ground.

At times I have to pinch myself, though, to find out if I'm dreaming the fact that I am still involved in international rugby at the age of 34, given that in my youth my main interests were those lurchers and terriers I used to tramp over the hills with. While other kids would collect stamps or bubblegum cards, I'd fill scrapbooks with details of different types of hunting dogs. I'd list the heights and weights of all the ideal lurchers as well as their respective qualities – greyhounds, Irish wolfhounds, Saluki, Scottish deerhounds, Bedlington terriers, borzoi and so on. You could learn from my notes, for example, that the Ibizan hound was the best jumper, while the Saluki would run all day. It's a passion which has never left me and was fuelled by the pup I bought through *Exchange and Mart* magazine many years ago. I'd worried for days beforehand about telling my Mum what I'd done, and I knew she would be particularly annoyed because we already had a Jack Russell. In fact, I hadn't got round to telling her when the dog was dropped off at our house in a tea-chest. As I had feared, Mum freaked out, but the cross terrier, to be duly named 'Skip', stayed.

Skip was part of the family too on the day I came home from school aged 15 and announced I was going out into the big wide world as an apprentice plumber the following Monday. I'd always intended to leave school at the earliest opportunity but two days before my 'escape' I had no idea what job I'd be entering. School held little attraction for me and although I was good with my hands at woodwork, metalwork and so on, technical drawing was a disaster. I used to copy from the guy sitting next to me, and on one occasion I even managed to pass an exam which he failed. Apparently my work was neater! A teacher offered me the chance of doing an 'O' level in technical drawing – or going into the horticulture class. I ended up digging the school garden and growing veg for the local old age pensioners.

I always thought about playing rugby league for a living, and it was no idle dream, because I was aware even then that in life you get few second chances and have to set out to achieve your goals. But I didn't have the nerve to put down 'rugby league pro' on the school careers form to indicate what I'd like to do for a living and instead chickened out by claiming I wanted to be a plumber or a farm worker.

On the Thursday before school was due to break for the summer holidays, the local plumbing firm, R.W. Charters, contacted the Kelso High careers master, saying they were looking for two apprentices. Since only myself and one other boy had expressed an interest in that type of job I found myself heading for an interview and being offered full-time employment. The following Monday, as my mates were embarking upon eight weeks' holiday, I was setting off for work with flask and sandwiches in hand.

I'd have loved that holiday, but there was work available which wasn't to be sneezed at. To this day I count myself fortunate never to have been unemployed. Well, that's if you don't count a situation I am almost too embarrassed to reveal and which occurred during my career at Widnes rugby league club.

With rugby league only being played on Sundays, some Widnes players cottoned on to the fact they were technically entitled to unemployment benefit through being available for regular employment on a Monday to Friday basis. Apparently there was a loophole in the law which said working on a Sunday didn't count as regular employment, so I went along and filled in what seemed like a batch of 500 forms to qualify for a special payment. Every week I reported to the local social security office and they asked me if I'd worked in the past week. Each time I replied, 'No, only on Sunday,' which was, of course, the truth.

I was getting £40 a week benefit, but what made things awkward was the fact that the more I played for Widnes, the more I could sense myself being recognised in the dole queue. It didn't feel right that I was earning £250 a win – and Widnes didn't lose very often – as well as my income supplement. Of course, I had to declare midweek games, but it was when a £400 Christmas bonus came through that my conscience really began to get the better of me. One day I dropped in to claim my entitlement and a bloke at the front of the queue was pleading that he couldn't afford to feed his kids, saying the poor wee souls were all starving. A woman was insisting she hadn't seen any of the money that the assistant was adamant had been paid out to her husband. As I stood at the back of the queue, surveying the scene, I suddenly thought, 'I'm getting out of this' – and literally ran from the room.

Soon afterwards Widnes took me on as a groundsman – my third 'real' job following on from plumbing and roofing. The roofing trade was something I more or less fell into when I realised I wasn't cut out for plumbing. The problem was that to qualify as a plumber I would have had to attend college in Galashiels on day release for three years. Sitting in a classroom was anathema to me, so I began to hang out with the roofers, who took me under their wing. Must be something to do with the outdoor life, I guess.

In switching trades I was fortunate to be able to stay with the same firm, who were always good at letting me away for rugby. To keep all the roofing apprentices on their toes, though, my boss, Wattie Charters, used to call upon the services of a retired slater who answered to the name of 'Pie' Lilley. 'Pie' used to teach us the tricks of the trade, but he was also very demanding. I'll vouch for that, because one day he looked at my work and said, 'Alan, those lines of tiles are as straight as a pigeon's beak.' It was probably a phrase 'Pie' used all the time and he could never have expected the ramifications to be quite so profound. The other apprentices fell about laughing and my put-down was the talk of the local building trade and spread over into Scottish rugby circles.

From that day onwards I've been known to some folk as 'Pidge', as in pigeon, and all because of that row of crooked roof tiles. Mind you, having been away in rugby league for a few years, I thought the nickname had been well and truly buried until Ian McGeechan, my coach at Scotland B level over a decade previously, revived it on the Lions tour of South Africa in 1997. It stopped me dead in my tracks suddenly to be referred to by someone in authority as 'Pidge' after all those years in rugby league where I was known by the highly unoriginal nickname of 'Taity'. I've always been flattered when people have been interested enough to quiz me as to how I came to be called 'Pigeon', but I've never let on as to the real origins. Until now. *The Scotsman*'s rugby diarist even invited readers to submit suggestions about how I came by the name, and most folk speculated it was because I had a barrel chest and long legs which made me walk like a pigeon. Apparently nobody got within miles of the correct answer.

Nicknames are a bonus in professional sport and help to give an individual an identity. But why couldn't I have had one like the Brazilian footballers? Pele, Zico or Socrates, maybe? They all sound so splendid. Romantic even.

'Pigeon' just doesn't have the same ring to it!

CHAPTER THREE

Poynder Pointers

Life is a learning experience and for six happy and informative years my classroom was Kelso rugby union club. Our ground at Poynder Park was often where I faced those twin impostors triumph and, occasionally, disaster, as the club gave me an urge for success and reminders of how to handle any that came my way. In that regard trophies were a handy accoutrement.

To begin with, triumphs on the 15-a-side front were rare, but seven-a-side tournaments hardly ever went past without Kelso being among the leading contenders. I grew up knowing the importance of having something to show for my exertions. I learned, too, how necessary it can be to let off steam with your mates without going over the top. And, on one occasion, I was slapped down and left in no doubt that an individual can never be more important than the team.

Charlie Stewart, one of twelve Kelso players before me who had represented Scotland, was club coach and he didn't take kindly to this young tyro turning up and demanding to be chosen only at centre and certainly not on the wing. All right, so I was making a bit of a name for myself as a decent prospect who had turned out for Scotland B. But that didn't excuse me from acting like a prima donna who could dictate the terms under which I deigned to play.

Charlie, a worldly-wise farmer, scythed me down to size by dropping me to the seconds, and because my pride was so offended that my heart wasn't in the task, I even descended into the thirds. That was when I received a kick up the backside and Jimmy Wilson, a club stalwart still turning out last season at the age of 53, was the man who delivered it. Jimmy talked some sense into my obstinate head. 'Get your act together, son,' he told me one day as we sat in the club lounge bar. 'Opportunities are passing you by.'

Of course, Jimmy was right, and I was soon back on the wing, to the approval of the local *Southern Reporter* newspaper which noted, 'Following his brief sojourn in the Kelso reserves, Alan Tait comes back into the Tweedsiders' line-up for the First Division game at Melrose – and he'll be turning out on the wing. It was the Scotland B three-quarter's original selection on the wing for the match against West which prompted Tait to opt out of the 1st XV. Kelso selectors have stuck to their guns and Tait has apparently patched up his differences with all concerned. As a member of the current Scotland squad and with two Scotland B appearances under his belt last season, for Tait to have stayed in the reserves would have spelt international suicide, and his reappearance for the Black and Whites' 1st XV will come as a big relief to supporters and officials alike.'

That wasn't my only run-in with the club and I also had to learn the importance of commitment to a cause – helped by a salutary reminder from my Dad. I had been due to play for Kelso's youth team, the Harlequins, in an away match at Langholm when the effort of getting out of bed had proved too much. Dad was in the public bar of the Black Swan Hotel when he learned from a friend, Pete Henderson, that the bus had left without me. Downing his pint, he sped home for a confrontation. Suffice to say the message was put across in no uncertain terms and I never again failed to show up for a match. Those were good times at the Quins thanks largely to Dave Thomson, another to whom I owe a special debt of gratitude.

On leaving school I drifted away from sport altogether and was more interested in hunting down every rabbit on the planet with my dog than scoring tries or making tackles. With Dad content to leave me to my own devices – so long as I wasn't breaking promises and letting people down – it was Dave who encouraged me to go along to the Harlequins, for whom I played my first game in a 34–0 win over Alnwick Colts on 10 October 1981. I'm aware of this, incidentally, thanks to the meticulous records kept by Ronnie Fleming, along with Glyn Hobkirk my first senior coach, on behalf of the club.

Ronnie maintains I was my own man in these days and I was fortunate he was prepared to tolerate my individualistic ways. Indeed, he revealed recently the extent to which he had his suspicions that I would not be seeing out my career in union, recalling how I sometimes had to be dragged away from any rugby league being televised in the Kelso clubrooms, even if training or a match beckoned.

It helped, of course, that the Quins were an above-average youth side who won more games than they lost, but even so the number of players who actually made it through our ranks and went on to enjoy a measure of senior success was limited. Together we ventured across the Irish Sea where, as part of a riotous weekend trip, we played a part in fostering Kelso's good relationship with the Dublin club Old Wesley. That was my first experience of touring.

Of my contemporaries, prop forward Garry Waite made it through to Scotland B level and winger Dougie Robeson turned out for the South of Scotland, while Neil Stewart, son of Charlie, was a useful all-round forward who starred in Kelso's Championship-winning side a few years later. But that was about it and David Thomson, despite being instrumental in getting me back in a pair of boots, will readily admit he never quite made the grade, although he did play a prominent role in the Kelso community as a key figure in the civic week celebrations that are part of Borders life.

As my first colts season reached the halfway point I found myself pushed up to the second XV, from where I graduated to the first XV for a try-scoring début in an 18–10 win over Jed-Forest in early January 1983, the first of 125 senior appearances. Playing with backs of the calibre of Andrew Ker, Ewan Common and Colin Flannigan, who was to set a Scottish points-scoring record for a single season, was a great experience, and we were never short of possession with the likes of John Jeffrey, Eric Paxton and Gary Callander in the forwards.

Kelso also had an outstanding seven-a-side team and for me it was simply a matter of finishing off what the inside players had created. Sevens are decried by a lot of people and I've even heard it said that sevens matches are to rugby what a church garden fête is to religion – a pleasant enough day out but nothing more. But, for me, playing sevens was always a chance to get my hands on medals and cups and generally cultivate that winning feeling. There can be no better sensation, and if a young player can be groomed in some kind of cup-winning tradition then so much the better.

I know that in Wales at one time there was a feeling that too much exposure to cups and medals early on left a generation feeling they had achieved all that could be achieved in rugby by the time they were in their mid-teens, and consequently they moved on to 'conquer' some other pastime. I don't subscribe to that theory. It disappoints me when I hear of kids returning home from mini-rugby tournaments without medals to recognise some attainment or other. The tangible evidence of having done well keeps children interested and provides something to show off.

I'd been knocking around the Kelso team for a couple of seasons, particularly enjoying a clash with my old friends from Cumbria, Glen Burgess and Tommy Borthwick, during a friendly match against Aspatria, when my big chance came in a star-studded charity match at Hawick on 28 March 1984. I suspect it was through my Dad's connection with Harry Whittaker, another former Workington rugby league player who lived in Hawick and a scrum-half considered unlucky not to aspire to the Scottish rugby union team, that I got my invitation to turn out.

Harry, who, when approached by Workington to leave Hawick, rendezvoused with his admirers on the fire-escape of a local Conservative Club so as to reduce the chances of being reported to the Scottish Rugby Union by eagle-eyed 'spies' and banned if any deal fell through, was to have a big bearing on my career in other ways too. He was one of the best osteopaths around, and there was many a time I beat a path to his door in search of treatment. Others from the north of England took my advice and followed the trail too. Ellery Hanley, the former Great Britain captain and coach, is one who owed a Challenge Cup final appearance at Wembley to Harry's healing hands. Martin Offiah and Shaun Edwards were others.

That Hawick charity encounter in aid of Cancer Relief and a shelter for handicapped people in India provided a chance to line up outside Jim Renwick, at the time Scotland's record cap-holder and once the world's most-capped centre, who on this occasion had been nominated at stand-off. If my boyhood sporting hero was tennis player Bjorn Borg – what a record he had at Wimbledon – when it came to rugby union players to follow in Scotland, Renwick was the best. Not only that but I loved his wry sense of humour. For example, intensely proud of his home town and dismissive of its main rival, he once proclaimed he'd rather be 'a lamppost in Hawick than the Provost of Galashiels'.

I was just one of several up-and-comings listed for the charity bonanza, among them a certain Gavin Hastings, later to captain the British Lions, and Iwan Tukalo, who also shared in Scotland's 1990 Grand Slam and became Scotland's most-capped winger. And the match itself? Talk about an armchair ride, as Renwick repeatedly spotted a gap and put me through as if he were threading a needle. I must have looked not too out of place in opposition to backs of the calibre of Roy Laidlaw, John Rutherford, Alastair Cranston, Steve Munro and Peter Dods, because the Scottish Under-21s soon came knocking for an international with Holland at Hilversum, and I was also invited to play for the South of Scotland side.

That début call left me with a bit of a dilemma – whether to play rugby for the South or watch my greyhound, Jack's Marvel, run at Powderhall Stadium in Edinburgh. Put it down as a sign of growing maturity (and ambition!) that I realised the importance of the rugby, and it was to prove a good day all round. Not only did the South of Scotland beat North and Midlands 44–6 on my home patch at Kelso, but Jack's Marvel romped in first at decent odds of 9–2!

One of the nice things about getting a foot on the representative ladder was the pleasure it appeared to give other folk who were following my career. For example, I have always treasured a couple of letters in particular. The first was from Tom Laing, then Kelso club president, who said, 'Just a short note to congratulate you on winning your Under-21 cap. I know you have played for the Under-21s before but I wanted to wait until you had played against another country and got what I imagine to be an international cap before writing. To be picked for your country you have to have something extra, and you have that something. Keep it up, and may you make many lasting friendships through rugby.'

My South of Scotland senior début prompted the following communiqué from Fiona Dagg, secretary of the Kelso supporters' club: 'I am writing on behalf of the supporters' club to congratulate you on your recent appearance for the South of Scotland. It has been a great pleasure to watch you in all the Kelso games, and the supporters' club appreciates your style of play. Having given a fine performance in your first outing for the South it can only lead to further deserved honours in the years to come. All the best for the future. Keep making the breaks and the breaks will come to you.'

Fiona's words proved prophetic because I was soon figuring in Scotland B line-ups, including a trip to Galway to face Ireland on a memorable day for Borders rugby. The fact it proved memorable was nothing to do with how we fared – the only thing people are liable to remember about the fixture is that Gavin Hastings somehow managed to miss the flight home – but the fact that the match coincided with the South of Scotland's 9–6 victory over Australia at Hawick.

From that outing, part of Galway's 500th anniversary celebrations, I continued in the B line-up for a trip to play Italy in Benevento, a match in doubt up until kick-off due to banks of fog rolling down from the mountains and shrouding the pitch.

Tour calls also arrived. I went with Scotland to North America in 1985 and along the Mediterranean to Spain and France the following year, although no caps were at stake on either venture. Touring with Scotland was something akin to being on automatic pilot, apart from training and playing. Everything was taken care of and it was mostly a case of showing up at the appropriate time wearing the appropriate clothing. We were 'processed' from rising in the morning until going to bed at night.

It was an altogether different scenario when I was called up at short notice to sit on the Scotland bench for a match with France at the Parc des Princes, Paris, in early 1987. Suddenly I was on my own in having to negotiate a journey which started when I was 30 feet off the ground mending a roof.

It was the Friday morning before the game and Roger Baird, my Kelso colleague, had apparently realised on wakening that an injury he'd been carrying was worse than first thought. An SOS call went out and so there I was, nailing down slates, when my boss appeared at the foot of the ladder, yelling up at me and insisting I had to get myself to Paris as quickly as possible but not to worry because everything would be laid on. At first I refused to come down off the roof to take the phone call, convinced it was a practical joke. When I asked who was on the line and my boss said it was Bill Hogg, SRU secretary, I knew he wasn't joking because he'd never have known to make that name up.

At the time I was driving a battered Fiesta which, for all its faults, was good enough to get me to Newcastle airport on the first stage of the journey. The trouble was I had no idea how to get to Newcastle by road (in rugby it is mainly a question of impressing Rob Andrew). After picking up some kit and making sure I was presentable in my Scotland tour blazer, I had to drop in on Caroline's workplace because she's always been good at pointing me in the right direction. It must be her training as a secretary.

At Newcastle airport I learned I was flying via Amsterdam, and at that stage I started to panic because I regarded myself as a country lad thrown out into a more frenetic world. The woman at the information desk where I collected my tickets tried hard to explain the procedure, but I couldn't take in a word she was saying. As it turned out, though, my spell in transit went smoothly and the Scotland tour blazer I'd chosen to wear paid handsome dividends on reaching Paris. There I was spotted by a couple of security guards who had been detailed to look out for me and I received an armed escort through the airport, past customs checks, and right up to the waiting Roger Baird, who had taken the trouble to greet me.

The Five Nations encounter passed without me being called off the bench and into the action, and I moved unsuspectingly into the dangerous part of the excursion. Never mind those big French forwards. A night out with the Scottish team at that time was liable to be much more damaging. Senior 'pros' John Rutherford and Roy Laidlaw said they'd look after me when the team went out to a nightclub following the official dinner, and because we were with some of the French players, celebrity status was guaranteed. Rutherford and Laidlaw may have gone down in the annals as one of the great halfback combinations, but their strengths didn't extend to keeping an eye out for the innocent abroad.

Every player had a label stuck on his lapel indicating that he was entitled to a free drink, which, in our case, came by the bottle. My round was a bottle of gin, but no sooner had I lurched to the bar than I was solo on the streets of Paris, attempting to head back to base. My nickname may be 'Pigeon' but on this occasion I had certainly lost my homing instinct! I vaguely remember wandering across one of those roundabouts which give drivers the illusion they are in a chariot race in the days of ancient Rome. Cars were tooting their horns all around me as I staggered to the traffic island. Fortunately a taxi driver took pity on me and I could have been home in a matter of minutes –

except that I blurted out the name of the Hotel Windsor when, in fact, we were staying in the Hotel Westminster. An easy, but expensive, mistake to make before the exasperated driver managed to drop me at my safe haven.

Such a drunken retreat couldn't have upset any officials because a few days later I was named in Scotland's party for the inaugural World Cup in New Zealand. More of that event later, but suffice to say the experience, where I won my first cap, set me up for a memorable season with a Kelso club eager to build on a Border League title captured for the first time since 1937. Scotland was the first country to introduce national club leagues back in 1973 and since then Kelso had fluctuated between the first and second divisions. Now we were putting together a side which had a real backbone of players who knew their way around.

It is sometimes said that a team needs a hard core of perhaps seven or eight players and the rest will respond to their prompting. Of course, such a situation is relative to the standard of the competition, but in Kelso's case we fitted that criterion and it was mainly a question of whether we had the mental resolve to win a title.

Among the players who made Kelso tick I must single out hooker Gary Callander and stand-off Andrew Ker. Gary is a hard taskmaster who took no prisoners either on the pitch or when he moved into coaching. He has a cussedness that sets him apart and his high standards are not universally appreciated. Not everyone could meet his demands during spells calling the shots at Haddington, Boroughmuir and, latterly, Gala. Occasionally I could see that from close quarters, for it was always a pleasure to repay Gary's early encouragement by accompanying him to training sessions to pass on tips to his charges. Gary would undoubtedly have had more than six caps (five as captain) had he not had the misfortune to be around at the same time as Colin Deans and also suffer a back injury which ended his career. Last season ended with Gary outside the game looking in, but I am certain that a major role in Scottish rugby awaits this deep tactical thinker.

Andrew Ker coached Watsonians to the 1998 Tennent's Velvet Scottish Premiership title, having moved to Edinburgh, where he has a teaching job, long before his career with Kelso ended. Arguably Scotland's finest ever sevens exponent, Andrew was the most astute of playmakers and I was delighted when he belatedly received a couple of 15-a-side caps. Many well beyond the Borders were upset when the Scottish selectors bypassed Andrew, who is also a Scottish cricket international, as replacement for the injured John Rutherford at the 1987 World Cup. Instead they plumped for the relatively unknown Richard Cramb from Harlequins, who had the strategic advantage of being located in nearby Australia, where he was on a club tour, when the emergency arose. In fact, Andrew is an inspiration to those who maybe feel that opportunity has passed them by, because he became Scotland's oldest rugby débutant when he turned out against Wales in Cardiff in 1988 aged 33.

What also appeals to me about him, incidentally, is his willingness to speak his mind, but he copped a few choice words from me when we both travelled with Scotland to the Australian Rugby Union's centenary sevens tournament in 1988. Andrew and some of the lads had been out on the town when they came across a life-size cardboard cut-out of the singer Tina Turner and promptly had their photographs taken alongside the star. They managed to convince me they'd been wandering around Sydney with Tina who was, they said, a big rugby fan. According to them Tina had even set aside tickets so that we might attend her concert. I was strung along for several hours, believing I was bound for a concert and a backstage party, when I overheard a couple of hotel receptionists, in on the scam, saying it was a shame that I was being taken for a ride. Fences must have been mended pretty quickly, though, because Scotland, reinforced by Paul Moriarty of Wales because of injuries, reached the final of those Sydney Sevens.

Alas, after beating Australia in the semi-final we lost to the All Blacks, but not before I was party to a superb piece of retribution arising from the previous year's World Cup. There, waiting in the tunnel before the quarter-final with the All Blacks, Fin Calder had found himself taunted by their winger John Kirwan. According to Kirwan, who was heavily into the verbals, we were wasting our time even taking the field and we would be on the night flight home. Calder had not forgotten the put-down and loves to relate the tale of how, during the Sydney Sevens, he had followed through with a tackle on Kirwan moments after he'd passed the ball and brought up his knee to inflict a bit of damage.

'Here,' protested the man the Kiwis dubbed JK, 'that was late.'

'Aye, you're right,' growled Calder. 'About a year late . . .'

But back to Kelso, and during that post-World Cup season we lost only once, notching some notable victories and achieving personal milestones. A 53–4 victory at Kilmarnock saw me land my first drop goal for the club, and I also got a hat-trick of tries.

The match which really indicated that it might be Kelso's season, though, came in the lead-up to Christmas when we won 32–3 at Watsonians. Colin Deans, my World Cup captain who had retired to the press box, wrote in the *Sunday Post*, 'It is becoming clear that Kelso have the composure, the personnel and the commitment to launch a serious assault on the Division One title.' David Steele told readers of *The Herald*, 'The second half was the Alan Tait show. The international centre gave a splendid display of running and when direct enough the tries came.' Finally, *The Pink* Saturday evening sports paper in Edinburgh was also impressed, noting, 'It is worth pondering whether there is a better centre in Britain right now than Alan Tait.'

So, Kelso reached the concluding match of the season without conceding a try at home in the league, and provided we beat Heriot's FP, and Hawick, our only conquerors in the league, did not run amok at home to Musselburgh, we would be crowned champions.

Of course, Kelso had ruled the roost before, but that was back in the 1947–48 season when the club championship had been based on newspaper-compiled merit tables distorted by the fact that teams did not play all their rivals. It was a far-from-perfect system but one which, in my view, still lent a much-needed competitive element thanks in no small part to the efforts of rugby writer Reg Prophit, then of the *Evening Dispatch*, who diligently compiled the table and ensured it was published. How the authorities must have hated such vision and pioneering spirit!

Victory over Heriot's FP was achieved by a resounding 35–0 but my rugby education was enhanced by an incident which still earns me rebukes to this day. Norman Mair noted in *The Scotsman*, 'Alan Tait threw away one try when, after Simon Edwards, Roger Baird, [Gary] Callander, [Marshall] Wright and Doug Robeson had brilliantly counter-attacked from a kick-off, he shrugged off the remnants of the defence but was so busy prematurely punching the air in triumph that he lost the ball as Henry Murray tackled him in the in-goal area. Yet, overall, Tait's strong running was frequently in evidence.'

In view of my flamboyant gesture on the way over the try-line I had a particularly anxious wait until the result from Hawick came through and we were confirmed as champions. No harm was done, and since I knew I had achieved a major goal before taking what I regarded as an inevitable journey into rugby league, I was in high spirits approaching the next target for the club – the Melrose Sevens.

On the day of the tournament I travelled to Melrose along with team-mates Andrew Ker and Roger Baird in a car driven by our coach, Charlie Stewart. I knew I would be moving on to league soon after and I was too busy cracking jokes and bantering to realise how wound up the others were about the immediate challenge that lay ahead. Suddenly I sensed I was out of order and by way of an apology I turned to Charlie and said, 'If you want to win the tournament so badly then we'll win it. Just you leave it to me.' With hindsight, it was another example of what some will maintain is cockiness. To me, though, the remark came spontaneously because I had such belief in the ability of others in the side as well as myself. The look in Charlie's eyes when I made my pledge has lived with me ever since, because he knew I meant what I said. Instantly Charlie appeared to relax and stopped preaching at me to adopt a more serious approach.

In the end it was one of the highlights of my Kelso career. I grabbed two tries to help take the final, against Jed-Forest, to extra time, and we eventually won. As acting captain I should have gone up to lift the trophy, but both Baird and Ker appealed to me to let Eric Paxton have the honour since he was due to retire at the end of that season. I didn't have a problem with that because I had one thing on my mind – and that had everything to do with visiting places like Featherstone, Wigan and St Helens in Widnes colours.

It was funny how the appeal on behalf of Eric came to mind again the following year when I was settled into my Widnes home and, because we played our matches on Sundays, was watching the final of the Melrose Sevens live on television. Who should be stepping forward to receive the trophy but Eric Paxton, who was supposed to have retired a year earlier! I thought, 'You old trouper,' but really I was anything but annoyed because Eric loved the Melrose Sevens and I think the crowds loved him. 'Eck the Dunt', they called him, because of his protruding Desperate Dan-type chin.

Besides, Eric was always a player I looked up to in my formative years at Kelso, perhaps because he was a bit different. Just as I was breaking into the Kelso team Eric had shown it was possible to gain international recognition whilst at our club by being capped against Ireland in Dublin, and he also had an unusual personal training regime which involved running and walking between alternate telegraph poles. People said he was crackers. In fact Eric was ahead of his time and preferred to cultivate sharpness than go in for the training slogs that represented conventional wisdom little over a decade ago.

There were other, older, Kelso stalwarts who also had major influences on my career and who are deserving of a mention. Few have made a more all-round contribution to rugby union in Scotland than Charlie Stewart. Besides playing at international level (winning two caps) and coaching his old club, Charlie also served as the Scottish Rugby Union president. That last appointment must have made it slightly awkward for him when, with professionalism looming in the 15-a-side code, he sought me out in rugby league for a chat about how Kelso should equip themselves. I thought a lot of Charlie for doing that because, to me, it conveyed his deep-rooted love of a club he was determined should not be left behind. Alas, the only answer I could give was that he should walk into the Kelso clubrooms where photographs of the club's internationals hang on the wall.

'Underneath each photograph,' I told Charlie, 'place a price tag.'

My point was that a small-town club like Kelso was unlikely to be able to compete with wealthier rivals in the cities, but if future John Jeffreys or Roger Bairds could be unearthed then it was important that they should be nurtured properly to bring out their potential – and subsequently the going rate on the transfer market.

John Dawson, as a rugby-playing sprinter of some repute, would have commanded a reasonable transfer fee had he played on the wing for Kelso today. Perhaps another Martin Offiah! Back in 1952 John won the venerable Powderhall Sprint, running under his mother's maiden name of Franklin – *noms de plume* are part of a professional running tradition – and the fact that he achieved such a feat meant he automatically had my respect when he began to coach me for a spell as a professional athlete.

On the day I turned professional with Widnes, John was one of the first people on my doorstep wishing me well. I suspect he knew early on that something like that would happen, because as a break from athletics training he would groom me for giving interviews on the grounds that one day I'd need to be able to sell myself and my sport. In short, John had faith in my abilities, and a young player especially needs that kind of support.

There was also a bit of a rebellious streak in John which I liked and which almost threw a substantial part of the athletics world into turmoil. It was after he'd won the Powderhall Sprint that John was serving as a private with the Royal Scots in Korea and competing on the Asian running circuit. In those days, apparently, the Japanese sprint championship, which he was encouraged to enter in the hope of bringing kudos to his regiment, was conducted on a grand prix basis with meetings held around the country. John duly covered himself in glory in around 20 races to be crowned All Japan sprint champion when it emerged that he had previously sprinted for money and so, under the sport's strict amateur rules, was responsible for ensuring all his rivals would be barred. Much diplomatic activity involving the colonel of John's regiment followed, I'm told, before the matter was hushed up sufficiently for the amateurs to be able to get on with their lives without fear of being tainted. John Dawson knew what he was about, though, and arranged to have his trophy shipped home as evidence of his success before the storm broke.

To this day I have adopted one of John's favourite sayings: 'You never lose it as a professional, you just stop doing it!' I took that to mean that technique always stays with you, and I believe John could still outsprint me – 30 years his junior – over a couple of strides!

John was originally from Jedburgh and, since he was one of the few in the know that I would be leaving Kelso for rugby league, he must have savoured my last appearance – a Border League decider against his home-town club which they won on neutral territory at Melrose. I was pleased for the Jed-Forest players, particularly my international colleague Roy Laidlaw, but disappointed that I had ended the Kelso chapter of my career as a loser, in stark contrast to how I'd started out – as a raw, naïve teenager but nevertheless one capable of picking up trophies.

Naïve? Judge for yourself from the following incident which

occurred on the way home from one of my first senior sevens tournaments, at Berwick. As a reward for winning the tournament, our team was promised a free meal at a hotel and, during the journey, a colleague boasted of an affair with one of the waitresses/barmaids. To heighten our intrigue he refused to divulge any further details. It was up to us to guess who his concubine was, he said.

I'd scarcely, if ever, eaten out, and, as if having to use the correct cutlery were not hard enough, selecting from a menu, as opposed to having my food placed in front of me, was something else to contend with. When the menu was circulated I distinctly heard my boastful pal say 'I'll have a steak Diane' and, naturally, I assumed he had let his guard drop.

Ever the smart ass and intent on causing maximum embarrassment, I quickly resolved that when it came to my turn I wouldn't need to consult with any menu. 'Hi, Diane,' I piped up. '—— has been telling us all about you and him and, by the way, I'll have a steak as well.' Fellow players dissolved into laughter at my expense.

At least rugby was continuing to broaden my horizons – even to the extent of teaching me the contents of an average hotel menu!

CHAPTER FOUR

The Widnes Years

To me rugby league is the most professional sport in the world. Well, most of the time, anyway . . .

The exception which proved the rule occurred back on 16 April 1987, when I was selected to play for Scottish Rugby Union President Doug Smith's XV against the Spanish national team on my home-town pitch at Poynder Park, Kelso. The match was part of the build-up to the inaugural World Cup a month or so later in New Zealand, which I would attend as one of four uncapped players in a 26-strong Scotland squad. It was a match the President's men won 27–17 and nothing unusual happened afterwards. Which is exactly why the encounter had such a profound bearing on my sporting life!

Earlier I had opened negotiations with St Helens rugby league club, who agreed to send representatives to watch me against Spain. If I impressed, the idea was for me to put pen to paper for manager Alex Murphy almost immediately. Shortly before kick-off the President's XV was subject to a back-line reshuffle and, as a consequence of Iwan Tukalo dropping out, I was switched from centre to winger and my jersey number changed from 13 to 11.

Even though I say so myself, I played a blinder and scored two of our three tries. But weeks went by and I heard nothing from St Helens. Eventually my Dad, drawing on his contacts as an ex-rugby league pro, called Alex Murphy. 'Your lad's too tall and too clumsy,' was Murphy's verdict, which came as a bombshell to Dad, who stuttered in reply, 'What do you mean, tall? He's only 5ft 11in.'

It appeared that the streetwise, hard-nosed St Helens club had, on this occasion, put their trust in a couple of scouts who were probably so excited at the prospect of a wild night out in Kelso that they didn't bother to check late team changes. They thought that Euan Kennedy, the 6ft 5in Watsonian centre who was wearing the number allocated to me in the programme, was me! To discourage further the deputation who never stood a chance of graduating from the M62 corridor to the clandestine world of MI6, Euan had the misfortune to set up the Spanish winger for a try when his pass was intercepted.

When rumours abounded of one top player, who became a British Lion in 1997, going from rugby union to rugby league and not being required to undergo a medical due to an oversight, some scoffed at the suggestion of such an occurrence with so much money at stake. But I believed it could easily happen in view of my own experience. Oversights do occur and, occasionally, rugby league clubs operate on a more haphazard basis than they'd care to admit even though many thousands of pounds may be riding on a signature.

Given that I went on to represent Great Britain 14 times at rugby league, I feel entitled to claim it was a costly blunder by St Helens to pass me by through lack of forethought. But just suppose their scouts had been on the ball? How would my rugby career have turned out, for in all probability I'd have jumped at an offer from St Helens and to hell with the rugby union World Cup which was a voyage into the unknown anyway?

Rugby union World Cups are high-profile events nowadays, but back then nobody knew how things would turn out and sponsorship was only secured at short notice when a Japanese computer firm, KDD, decided to provide backing. Besides, the home unions had to be dragged to the party by more progressive counterparts in Australia and New Zealand, who had rugby league to keep them on their toes.

The likelihood, so far as I am concerned, is that I'd never have been capped by Scotland if the representatives of the Knowsley Road club had been up to speed. And there would have been no, dare I say, 'second coming' to Murrayfield all those years later. Certainly, even if I had managed to get myself in the Five Nations frame after a spell in league, there wouldn't have been anything like the same excitement in the media because I'd have been a much less well-known figure.

St Helens' favour was something I had been courting because at that time I was taking more and more interest in rugby league. This enthusiasm stemmed not only from my father's past involvement but also from the fact that the fabulous Australian Kangaroos were in the country. Part of my childhood was spent stretched out on the living-room carpet watching matches involving Wally Lewis, Peter Sterling and Ray Price, who all became heroes. To remind me of their special talents I'd record games on a battered old Betamax video machine, and I remain convinced that detailed examination of the superstars is the ideal way to learn.

When Ike Southward, a former colleague of my Dad's at Workington Town, phoned to ask if I was the same Alan Tait who used to knock around the Cumbrian Schools rugby scene I was excited at the prospect of getting a signing offer. I was flattered, also, to be noticed by somebody with Ike's pedigree. Once Britain's costliest player when he moved from Workington Town to Oldham for £10,650 and on two occasions part of a winning Great Britain squad in an Ashes series with Australia, Ike knew his stuff. I later learned, too, that he was a regular visitor to the Borders on 'spying' missions, mostly to Hawick in those days. Targets included Jim Renwick and Alastair Cranston as well as, much later, Tony Stanger, while he swears that his former chairman at Workington Town, Tom Mitchell, was in dialogue at one time or another with my old Kelso colleague Roger Baird and even Andy Irvine, a triple British Lion and now chairman of the SRU's high-powered International Committee.

Roger's representatives are supposed to have discussed terms at a pub in Canonbie while he waited in a car outside *en route* to a match in Blackburn. Those who mock the idea of a former public schoolboy like Roger playing rugby league should remember that Martin Offiah is the son of a judge! Having said that, it was once suggested, no doubt apocryphally, that Gavin and Scott Hastings could never have gone 'north' because their Dad, Clifford, would have been drummed out of the posh Honourable Company of Edinburgh Golfers based at Muirfield for having a son associated with rugby league!

On his own admission Ike Southward never had much success in luring Scots to league, but his raids did not always go unrewarded – on one occasion he travelled to Hawick to watch Jim Renwick and returned home with a bottle of sherry after winning the traditional half-time raffle.

My Dad told Ike that I was beginning to climb the ladder in rugby union and, yes, I did fancy playing rugby league. At this time, though, Workington were struggling and couldn't afford any expensive signings, but Ike said he would put the word about down the M62 corridor, which is where the action was to be found anyway, so far as I was concerned – no disrespect to Cumbria intended!

Clearly Saints had their ear to the ground and their interest was renewed just prior to the start of the 1988 Five Nations Championship. First, though, they wanted me to go down on trial but my Dad intervened, saying that if rugby union authorities got wind of the scheme I'd be thrown out of the sport on my ear with no bargaining power. There was nothing to be gained by me, now an established international, playing a trial. In fact I would have had a considerable amount to lose, because I might have ended up having to sign for virtually nothing, just to maintain an active interest in rugby.

Years later I attended a Sportsman's Dinner at which Alex Murphy was guest speaker, and afterwards he invited questions. Seizing my chance, I asked Alex why he didn't come and get me for St Helens when I was ready to jump. Alex remembered tracking me and even went on television after I'd signed for Widnes and very kindly remarked that one of the biggest mistakes he had made in management was not signing me. Alex also explained that he had begged the St Helens board to back his judgement, knowing I wouldn't play a trial because I needed to retain the option of playing rugby union. But they said they couldn't give him the money that was required without seeing the 'goods' on display, no matter that I'd faced the All Blacks, French and so on in the 15-a-side code.

Fortunately for me a short article had appeared in the *Liverpool Echo* to the effect that Alex Murphy was trailing a young Scottish rugby union international and indicated, 'Watch this space.' Doug Laughton, the Widnes coach, doesn't let grass grow under his feet and, having been tipped off through reading the newspaper, dived in while Alex Murphy and St Helens prevaricated. Laughton even rolled up at my door in a Widnes rugby league club sponsored car covered in stickers proclaiming his identity. So much for the cloak-and-dagger approach of the hard-nosed pros!

Laughton had a bit more scope to negotiate than Murphy had done and offered a deal which made out that my signing would be a gamble for him and for me. The offer was for over ten years, which I now know is a ridiculous length of time to commit yourself to a club. However, when somebody comes along and offers a youngster

£85,000 tax paid, I suspect most are going to take it. Especially as my 'agent', i.e. my Dad, had told me to bite at any offer in the region of £30,000 to £40,000. It emerged that Dad was well out of touch with the market and was still thinking in terms of payments when he was playing.

Anyway, we sat in the living-room of my house while Caroline, my wife, cooked Doug a meal. Doug asked me what sort of money I was looking for to sign, and I honestly didn't know where to start. He said, 'I'll tell you what. I'll give you the same as the rest of the ex-rugby union players I've signed, including Martin Offiah.' Having skilfully dropped a high-profile name into the conversation to show he placed me in the same bracket, he explained that that would be £8,500 a year guaranteed, plus a £250 cash bonus per win with the club paying the tax. Over and above that there would be increments for success in any cup competitions, with financial rewards too for being picked to play representative matches for Great Britain.

I decided against signing on the spot only because Scotland still had to play England in the Five Nations, but I must admit I was enjoying my rugby union and if I had resisted for much longer I could easily have been lured by some of the glamour trips available from Murrayfield. However, that final match of the season against England turned out to be one of the worst games of rugby I have ever played in, as the auld enemy mauled their way to a 9–6 win. Afterwards Derrick Grant, the retiring Scotland coach, accused the English of being boring, and it was hard not to sympathise with his view.

At the team hotel prior to the official dinner I went with Caroline to have a drink with Roy Laidlaw, who had retired from international rugby that day, and his wife Joy. Roy was on a real downer, and if I had any doubts about going to rugby league, one look at his face was sufficient to convince me I should sign for Widnes. I thought to myself, 'I don't want to hang around and maybe collect 50 caps before ending up as miserable as Roy on the day his international career finished.'

Having resolved to sign for Widnes, I was pleased to learn from my Dad that Doug Laughton would be in the Borders the following Tuesday. I actually asked Doug to wait until I had played for Kelso in the Melrose Sevens, which we duly won, as well as a Border League title play-off with Jed-Forest the following Tuesday before signing. Looking back, I suppose I was subjecting myself to unnecessary injury risk with the money as good as in my bank account, but such is the innocence of youth!

Doug Laughton duly appeared on my doorstep the day after that Border League decider, which Kelso lost, and I signed. My Dad, who had left the room coughing and spluttering when the original sum of £85,000 had been agreed because he couldn't believe I had been so lucky, as he saw it, stayed this time, his face wreathed in smiles. As for Doug, he now claims he could have got me to sign for £50,000, but since the board had sanctioned him to go up to £90,000 I guess everybody was happy.

Before the ink was dry on the contract Doug went straight out to a telephone box and called Radio Mersey in order to milk the moment. I was fascinated by the emphasis Doug put on creating favourable publicity for Widnes. Unlike in union, where publicity of any sort was treated with suspicion, Doug realised that news of a signing which he hoped would strengthen a squad already with a League Championship trophy fresh on the sideboard was guaranteed to be well received back on Merseyside. The message Doug was keen to send out was that Widnes were not prepared to rest on any laurels – and why not flaunt their intentions in an effort to make opposition, who perhaps didn't have money to spend, feel inferior? Besides, I had a bit of a high profile from the Five Nations series and rugby league fans would like the idea of taking somebody with a bit of talent away from a code many of them despised for its holier-than-thou attitudes. Raa-raa rugby, they called union in those days! I had learned my first lesson as a professional, namely, always try to get an edge on the opposition.

Doug swears I'd have signed for a box of chocolates and jumped in the car alongside him to head south immediately. He's right. I would have done. But it wasn't that straightforward. First I had to set in motion the mechanics of trying to sell my house before I could get down to Widnes for what remained of the season. Such detail duly attended to, Widnes put me up in a hotel which I enjoyed until Doug Laughton ordered me out and into a flat with Martin Offiah.

Talk about going from riches to rags, because Martin always kept the heating turned down low and rarely had any food in the fridge.

When, eventually, I protested to Doug, he told me the upheaval had been necessary because I was spending £200 a week on drink and occasionally food as well! It was an astronomical sum and I was dumbfounded by the suggestion. But Doug gave me an old-fashioned look, smiled, and said, 'Come on. You know what I'm on about.'

I genuinely didn't have a clue what he was suggesting, but a few inquiries revealed that others in the Widnes team had been doing their drinking on my room tab after I'd gone to bed. What's more, champagne was a favourite tipple of my new 'friends', among whom Andy Currier was a prime suspect!

That, though, was just one part of the learning process. One hotel in Widnes was a particular haunt of the team, not least because it was always possible to bribe the chef for some nosh at odd hours when the kitchen was officially closed by producing a joint of cannabis. Some of the overseas contingent made a habit of smoking dope after every game and it was easy to get the chef to rustle up a meal, often at 4 a.m., if things were really going with a swing.

Of course, I worried about what would happen to them if any drug-testing unit pitched up at the club. I listened intently as they told naïve, innocent me of an alleged trick designed to fool the drug tester. Legend had it they cheated by taking a mouthful of water before letting the liquid run down their body via the chin until this 'river' reached journey's end at the specimen container. Or so they maintained . . . It goes without saying that anybody who tried this must have had their back to the drugs official and, of course, the testing laboratories were bound to be able to tell the difference between good old tap water and urine!

Clearly, though, I was among the more streetwise citizens and also granite-hard men, as I had quickly discovered on turning up for my first training session. What a nightmare experience that session was to prove for a relatively shy country lad like myself, not least because I could sense disappointment on the part of my new colleagues when I entered the Widnes dressing-room. Wires had been crossed and the players were expecting a 6ft 5in and 17st goal-kicker – yes, exactly, someone of the build of Euan Kennedy who had been studied and rejected by St Helens. By comparison with the St Bernard they had been expecting, I must have registered as a Chihuahua. Joe Grima, one of the New Zealand contingent, voiced the general surprise, saying, 'Here – you're not the player we thought you were.' And I hadn't even pulled on a pair of boots at my new club. Some start!

It wasn't the players' faces that made the first impression on me, though, but something else entirely. Rather it was the smell of hard graft manifested in stinking, sweaty kit. I knew instantly I was among men not afraid of honest toil. The Widnes dressing-room was tidy enough, with everybody allocated individual lockers. But the air was heavy with perspiration.

The other thing that struck me was the lack of introductions. There was nothing formal whatsoever on my arrival. No grand announcement. Zilch. Save for the fact that I was allocated a locker next to Martin Offiah. There was certainly no gentle breaking-in of the new recruit, either. On the contrary, I will remember that first training session with Widnes until my dying day because of the way Doug Laughton flogged me almost mercilessly. Doug knew I could play rugby. After all, he had seen the tapes of my matches for Scotland. But he was determined to find out on the training field just how far I was prepared to push myself in order to be a success in the alternative code.

I'd just come off a Five Nations Championship but nothing I'd done there could ever have prepared me for that first day at Naughton Park. I hung over railings being sick as the first session ended in ignominy and my excuses to Doug Laughton about being out of sorts on account of being dazzled by the sun on the drive south cut no ice. 'Look, cock,' Doug told me. 'I've got enough liars at this club already without you adding to them.' What's more, a lot of the Widnes lads knew I was being tested out but they didn't let on, pretending the session was very much the norm.

Equally new to me were the training methods which comprised hitting tackle bags, then running at tackle shields. Drive the legs. Hit the bag. Drive the legs. Hit the bag. It was a monstrous grind. All this was hard enough at any time, but as a newcomer I felt nervous as well. The upshot was that my head started to spin, making me physically sick, and the grass came up to meet me as I collapsed in a corner. Then, as I began to come round, I could hear the Widnes players congratulating each other and saying well done on an exhilarating training session as the sweat flowed from them.

Widnes didn't have a specialist fitness trainer which, in retrospect, was maybe no bad thing for them and me. I learned from the outset about setting my own standards. Personal responsibility, and all that. Besides, you can't always rely on a fitness coach being in attendance. As for being an exhilarating session, well, it was pure murder for me. But for my fellow players those types of session seemed to be the norm – or so they convinced me.

As I lay on the floor I became aware of Kurt Sorensen, the Widnes skipper and a hard man of Danish/Tongan origin, standing over me. Kurt wanted to do a warm-down while I wanted to puke. But Kurt was the captain. The boss. If he said jump, players jumped. That was another lesson I learned on day one. Even by that early stage of my Widnes career I had become aware that Kurt was a man of few words, but when he looked down and told me to 'Get up', I still didn't know how to take it. He must have seen the quizzical look in my eye because he suddenly mellowed and began to communicate: 'I don't want you lying there. I just don't want you beaten.' I didn't know what he meant at first but later I realised it was a pride thing and Kurt, as captain, couldn't allow any of his team to exhibit a weakness. Ever.

My Dad had taught me years earlier never to show you are injured, or at least to disguise the real cause of concern, so that the opposition won't have a target to aim at. I drew encouragement from the fact Dad had been right all the way so far and that I had indeed been well schooled in the professional ways. I got up and jogged round with Kurt and the lads, warmed by a feeling that with the background preparation I'd had I might make it after all in rugby league.

Once the warm-down was over Kurt came up, tapped me on the shoulder and said 'Well done', which meant I had taken a small step towards earning a bit of credibility, if not yet respect. It was clear, too, that Kurt didn't want Doug Laughton, who was in the far corner, to see he had cracked any player, for, having done that, others might be targeted to see how far they could be pushed.

If Kurt Sorensen was helping me, he wasn't doing so in a sympathetic, patronising way, which was important. He did it in a tough way, as he always did things, but I had got through that session with a bit of self-esteem entirely through a willingness to carry on to the bitter end. Kurt played tough and wanted me to harden up, and it was more a mental issue so far as he was concerned, with self-discipline the name of the game. Rightly so.

Amazingly, from my point of view – and those of a number of team-mates, no doubt – I went straight into a first-team match the following weekend. I couldn't understand the rush because I hadn't even had a game of any description. My team-mates were entitled to be concerned for their bonuses, considering only two substitutes were permitted and I, a complete novice, was one of them. My début was a Premiership first-round tie against Halifax, a team now known as the Blue Sox. They weren't a bad side, as you'd expect considering the competition is open only to the top eight teams in the league.

Widnes put me on for the last ten minutes, and even in that short space of time and feeling my way around I found the speed of the game unbelievably fast. As an *hors d'oeuvre* for what lay ahead down the years, I received a whack around the mouth when bursting on to a short ball. Absorbing the impact of the blow I felt my legs turn to jelly, and as I looked up I made eye contact with my Mum. The trouble was I couldn't focus. My eyes seemed to be going in different directions. Afterwards my Mum offered a sympathetic but deeply concerned ear, saying, 'You were hurt, weren't you?' Sensing she might not be too enamoured with my chosen career and might start putting doubts in my head, I mumbled something in reply along the lines of 'At least I didn't go down' and quickly moved away. But she was right. Mums usually are.

The final whistle brought victory for Widnes and congratulations all round. More importantly, in view of the life I had chosen to lead and the blow I had just taken, my first bonus cheque was on its way to the bank.

Following that outing there was just one opportunity to play for the seconds before their season ended, and the match was against Hull Kingston Rovers, coincidentally coached by George Fairbairn, who had left Kelso some 15 years before me for a career in rugby league. Widnes seconds won 84–0 in a fixture which left me puzzled for some time afterwards. What I couldn't get my head round was the fact that as I crossed for a try the Hull KR full-back, who had put in a desperate and unsuccessful attempt to stop me, said, 'Well done, Taity.' I had expected a tough game and certainly no such friendliness. When the same thing happened following my second try, I began to feel thoroughly bemused. Come full-time I learned that Doug Laughton had left, apparently well satisfied with his investment, but Paul Lansbury, our kit man, was still around. I told Paul about the congratulations I had received and he rocked with laughter. 'You daft git, Taity,' he said. 'Some of your opponents were Widnes players. Hull KR only turned up with eight men and we had to lend them a few to fill in, otherwise the fixture would have been called off.'

Suddenly it all fell into place. The renegades on the Hull KR side hadn't been tackling. They had been letting me go through. To this day I don't know who they were, but I have to thank them for contributing to my 'man of the match' award which did so much to build early confidence.

Next up came Warrington in the Premiership semi-final, and what an eye-opener that proved to be. Just before half-time Martin Offiah got injured and I was off the bench and on the pitch when a massive brawl erupted 'live' on national television. Why, it was so Wild West-ish that a spectator even got headbutted by a player. I kept out of the 'action' even though I was only 20 yards away, but my discipline actually earned me a rollicking. Mike and Steve O'Neill, brothers who played for Widnes, rebuked me for not getting stuck in and left me wondering for about the only time in my career if I had made a mistake going into rugby league.

At least Widnes won and I found myself looking forward to a final at Old Trafford, no less, home of mighty Manchester United. For the final I was on the bench, and the decision to list a rookie as substitute was certainly widely queried, since the national spotlight had swung heavily on to Widnes for the first time since my arrival. Our opponents were St Helens, who had just finished second to Widnes in the league and whose manager, Alex Murphy, had wanted to buy me from rugby union before running into problems with his directors.

Murphy's Saints were out for revenge on Laughton's Chemics, as we were nicknamed, for the loss of the league title, and as an added pressure it had been announced that the 'coach of the year' accolade would hinge on the outcome. That, to me, seemed unfair and a bit of a cop-out. But it was a clear indication of what was at stake.

Seven minutes into the game our winger Rick Thackray went down after falling on a rough patch of ground and injuring his groin. The pitch at Manchester United looks immaculate any time I see it on television now, but in those days it was heavily sanded, especially towards the end of the season, and what happened to Thackray could

have occurred two or three times. But it's an ill wind and all that . . .
Seventy-three minutes after going on I had my first winner's medal,
having scored a try to boot. It was to prove the first of many rugby
league medals and golden experiences.

As a curtain-raiser to Widnes's 1988–89 campaign we went to play
Wigan on the Isle of Man in a Charity Shield tie, and out of the blue
Doug Laughton asked if I fancied playing full-back. Well, I might
have been a rugby league rookie but I also knew it was impossible to
refuse a manager's request. Not that I had any intention of doing so,
for anything that would get me a regular slot in the starting line-up
was worth considering. Doug explained that he already had two good
centres in Andy Currier and Darren Wright, both of whom stood
over 6ft and weighed around 15 stone. That, to me, was tantamount
to saying there was a fast track to the first team available if I cared to
take the chance being offered.

It was in at the deep end, for Wigan's last line of defence was none
other than Steve Hampson, the Great Britain stalwart. I must have
done okay in the match, though, because soon afterwards Doug
Laughton's assistant coach, Colin Tyrer, put in a good word for me as
a full-back following a match at Halifax. I had found my optimum
berth and, as far as I was concerned at least, there was no going back
to centre as long as I was in rugby league. We lost that day at Halifax
when Tyrer did so much to boost my ego but it was there, in the car
park at Thrum Hall, that I learned a lesson that would sustain me
throughout my professional rugby career.

Kurt Sorensen, for one, had a big influence on Doug simply
because the boss knew which players would almost have died for him
and the club. So, it was the same when it came to playing the transfer
market, and Doug would ask some of the more experienced cam-
paigners if such and such an individual had the mental strength to do
a job for the club. The senior pros could put the black ball in and,
similarly, if they turned round and pointed the finger at someone who
wasn't pulling his weight, he was gone. Simple as that.

When Doug told me he was thinking of signing Jonathan Davies,
I was sceptical about the chances of the Welsh wizard moving. But
Doug assured me it was a possibility, and I encouraged him further
by enthusing over the talents I had first seen in a rugby union match
at Heriot's FP in Edinburgh. Jonathan was playing for a select team

called the Co-Optimists and I had the privilege of being asked to play outside him. The Co-Optimists – the name was taken from a pre-war music-hall act – put 60-odd points past Heriot's FP and much of the damage was done by Jonathan, who had insisted on bringing with him a scrum-half of his choice. Andy Booth was the player entrusted with providing the right kind of service, and Jonathan's *pièce de résistance* was a try from the shadow of his own posts after taking possession from a lineout and dancing off his left foot inside the opposing stand-off.

I told Doug, 'Jonathan's got everything skill-wise – and enough self-esteem that he picks his own scrum-half whenever he is allowed to.' Indeed, so far as talent and speed were concerned, Jonathan really was phenomenal. Something else entirely. What I didn't know was whether he had the bottle or the attitude to adjust and re-learn part of his craft having been put on a pedestal in South Wales for so long. Doug assured me that from what he had seen on video tapes, Jonathan most certainly had the mental strength, so I urged him not to hang about, saying, 'If you're sure about his bottle then he's going to be some player in rugby league.'

The deal was done within weeks. Doug Laughton really doesn't let the grass grow under his feet. The question was: who would be displaced by Jonathan once he had eventually settled in league? As it turned out, he spent his first year of rugby league on the wing, mainly for his goal-kicking, and Doug kept on signing players. Paul Moriarty arrived from rugby union and Emosi Koloto rolled up from the southern hemisphere, both on account of Doug Laughton's remark-able ability to make the correct soundings.

In the case of Moriarty, who was based in South Wales, Doug found it hard to get an honest assessment of the player's ability and attitude from people who knew him well. Word was out that rugby league were interested, and with Welsh rugby in a perilous state through 'defections', the drawbridges were up. League scouts were spotted a mile off. To achieve a breakthrough, Doug rang an escort agency and hired a couple of girls who were paid to infiltrate a group of Swansea club officials and primed to remark in their company that the 'big blond number eight [Moriarty] was rubbish'. The girls duly reported back that they had been told they didn't know what they were talking about and that Moriarty was the best player the club had.

Doug paid his dues to the modern-day Mata Haris and in return had the confirmation he was looking for.

Obtaining the signature of Koloto meant a journey to New Zealand for Doug and Widnes chairman Ray Fox. They went straight from the airport to a game in Wellington which had kicked off 20 minutes before their arrival at the ground. As luck had it, Koloto retired with a broken nose just before half-time and the likelihood of him playing again during Doug's stay was slim. Undeterred, Doug marched into a crowd of fans and asked in a loud voice, 'What's happened to the big, soft, useless bastard who was hurt a minute ago?' The ploy worked a treat, for Doug claims to have been submerged by invective as well as – thankfully – cries of 'What do you mean, soft – he's the hardest guy we've got!'. I'll vouch for Emosi's hardness, having gone on fishing trips with him during the Widnes pre-season training camps on Anglesey, in North Wales. There I've seen him sit down and eat mackerel from a bucket without bothering to chop off the heads or tails. Yuk. That man has an iron constitution.

Once again, though, Doug, a keen student of psychology who claims to have read shelves of library books on the subject to help him cut corners in his search for an education and a business edge, had turned up trumps. Doug also prides himself, incidentally, on being able to spot a troublemaker in a crowded room – a knack which contributed enormously to the happy team spirit at Widnes. With the arrival of the rugby union legions, a lot of the local lads were asking serious questions about the road down which the club was travelling, but we all mixed in well. When Jonathan arrived, Tony Myler, for example, must have wondered, as a stand-off, what the future held for him. It is a tribute to Tony that he retained the berth and, as he said at the time, it didn't matter where the arrivals came from just so long as we were all there for the same thing – the greater good of Widnes.

I'm convinced that anybody who moves to rugby league purely for the money doesn't last long. The camaraderie in that Widnes team was incredible, and I'm proud of the fact that we produced things that I'm told had rarely been seen in rugby league before. We'd have been even better had Doug Laughton succeeded with an audacious bid to sign David Sole just after he'd captained Scotland to a Grand Slam in 1990. Approaches were made while David was on the tour of New Zealand which followed that year's Five Nations campaign, but the former Bath star wasn't interested. Pity. Few forwards make the transition to league but David's mobility and ball-handling skills might have made him one of the exceptions.

As a basis for the sense of adventure and improvisation that was the Widnes hallmark, Jonathan Davies, Martin Offiah and I could all run 100 metres in under 11 seconds. Nobody would kick the ball in league on the first tackle and it was always a matter of taking the ball up and probing for openings. I like to think we revolutionised things when Tony Myler started to chip the ball over the top of the advancing defence for us to run on to. Why it hadn't been tried much earlier baffled me, because at a scrum the defending side would invariably line up straight in front of the attacking team on a man-for-man basis, with nobody sweeping up behind them.

Our chip-and-chase tactic created heaps of tries, especially for Martin Offiah, who would probably have been of Olympic sprint standard had he put his mind to it. With Martin around I could take the winger and full-back out of the game and slip the ball inside. He would always be there. He was the only player who would still be on my shoulder if I ran full pelt through a gap, and he once gave me a bit of credit on BBC's *Grandstand* for laying on many of his scores. It was reassuring to know I could stop running after offloading to him in the sure knowledge he would be in under the sticks.

At Widnes we also brought in fancy moves from rugby union off the back of the scrum. We produced loop moves and mis-moves to slice teams open and the crowds rolled up, although you might be hard-pressed to get many of them to admit to the fact that rugby union, where such practices were more common, contributed to a revival of the 13-a-side code! Old rivalry and bitter prejudice isn't that easily brushed aside.

It was so very, very unfortunate that Widnes never got to Wembley and a Challenge Cup final during the time we were together, despite being in three semi-finals. In fact, during my spell with the club we won a League Championship, three Premierships, a Regal Trophy, three Charity Shields and a Lancashire Cup in addition to the World Clubs' Challenge. But I might even have swapped one of my two Harry Sunderland Trophies given to the 'man of the match' in a Premiership final for a Wembley appearance with Widnes.

On the first occasion I reached a Challenge Cup semi-final St

Helens were the opposition and Richie Eyres got sent off within ten minutes, leaving Widnes to play the remainder of the match with 12 men. Even then we were within ten minutes of going through when Saints got a winning try in the corner through Les Quirk. If Widnes had got to Wembley that year then there might have been money in the pot to keep the players. As it happened a break-up was looming, but at least I shared in Premiership and League Championship triumphs, not to mention that World Clubs' Challenge final win over the Canberra Raiders at Old Trafford, when we won 30–18 after falling a dozen points behind in the first 11 minutes. Years later Doug Laughton was still highlighting that match as an example of how guts can prevail if a team is determined enough to play until the final whistle. That night Canberra took the field for a warm-up and were so confident they even indulged themselves in a series of ball-juggling exercises. Doug reckoned we were a bit mesmerised to begin with, but we then got stuck in to produce the right result.

There's a lot of bull talked, incidentally, about the southern hemisphere superiority in league as well as union – something that is skilfully exploited to psyche teams out. Sure, they take rugby more seriously down under. But a lot of their drive stems from a deep-rooted desire to put one over on the old 'mother country', and sport is the vehicle that provides the opportunity to do just that. Match their will to win and you are well on the way to bridging any gulf, and, remember, the Widnes team that won the World Clubs' Championship did so on the back of training two nights per week plus a Saturday morning of fine-tuning for the game the following day. As rugby union is discovering, over-training players can be far more debilitating than under-cooking them.

Winning a World Clubs' Championship with Widnes was obviously a source of immense pride to me and showed what can be achieved against the southern hemisphere when the attitude is right. I was particularly proud of that result, and proud, too, of the fact that my Dad used to watch Widnes in the halcyon days of the late 1980s and early 1990s and always said he loved coming down from the Borders because of the quality of our play. That was some tribute, because it was an effort for him to bring himself to negotiate the mile or so along the road from his home to Poynder Park, Kelso.

Maybe it was not so surprising, though, that Dad's rugby preferences lay in the north of England. When I was growing up and playing rugby union, he'd always say that rugby league players would show me how things were done. These guys provided Dad with his yardstick, and one match in particular which left him drooling was a winner-take-all Stones Bitter Championship decider against Wigan at our home ground, Naughton Park, when a crowd of 20,000 created a unique atmosphere. Widnes won 32–18 and a month or so later I had added to a fairytale first full season in rugby league by capturing the Harry Sunderland Trophy when we wrapped up the Premiership by beating Hull. The following year I retained that man-of-the-match cachet when we defeated Bradford, the first player to do so.

Another memorable encounter which will live long with me was the 24–0 Widnes victory over Leeds at Central Park in the 1992 Regal Trophy final. Rugby league reporter Ian Proctor summed up the achievement, saying,

> Widnes turned back the clock – and breathtakingly turned on the style – to lift the Regal Trophy for a third time in their record eighth final appearance. And the second Trophy success under Frank Myler, coming 16 years after the wily old campaigner's first, must have made painful viewing for the team's maker, Doug Laughton. He could only watch as Widnes humiliated his new charges.
>
> With Martin Offiah transferred to Wigan, a side short of David Hulme, Emosi Koloto, Esene Faimalo, Tony Myler, Paul Moriarty and the dropped Phil McKenzie, and Laughton in the opposite dug-out, this Trophy decider was as much a test for the new-look Widnes as it was for the resurgent Leeds. And Widnes were outsiders to win the competition for the first time since their four-cups season of 1978–79.
>
> Typically, Widnes proved they can win trophies by digging deep and resurrecting the amazing team spirit that has been prevalent at Naughton Park throughout their history. Against the odds, they produced a wholehearted team effort which swept favourites Leeds off their feet – and the record 24–0 victory margin would have been greater had the Chemics not had three first-half tries disallowed . . .

As my Widnes career was drawing to a close, I certainly had no regrets about my decision to leave rugby union and enter rugby league. As I told rugby league reporter Trevor Hunt, 'When Doug Laughton came to me with his offer I was flattered, but I also knew it was the chance that, really, I had been waiting for.' As I also said to Bob McKenzie of the *Daily Express*, 'The concentration on ball skills and tackling makes for better rugby at high speed, and I get far more freedom to play than I did at home because of the different styles. I like to tuck the ball under my arm and go. They want that here. But not so much in rugby union. You also need to be hard, to be able to get slapped around a bit and to give as good as you get.'

It always struck me as a bit strange that not more Scots followed me into league. I was frequently asked about the reasons for this by reporters. Once, after a period of reflection, I replied, 'Maybe it is harder for Scots to up their roots and move. A lot of players up there see rugby league on television and see how much harder it is; not in the sense of being dirty but just tough tackling, and it frightens them off. That's where it helped me to have some sort of background in the game.'

Derby matches at Warrington and St Helens always seemed very familiar to me too because of the atmosphere being very much like going with Kelso to play at Jed-Forest. Again, as I told Mike Chisholm of the *Southern Reporter* on the first anniversary of my move, 'Every game is a pressure game. There are no friendlies. You only play for points and money. You have to work on all parts of your game, especially strength and speed. I'm always on the weights. Weights were something I never used in rugby union. Whenever I can, too, I put my spikes on for sprint training. I need that to keep up with Martin Offiah, the fastest rugby player I've come across, regardless of codes.

'I wouldn't recommend the change for forwards unless they are prepared to work very hard. I've never seen forwards train the way they do in league. They eat training, running here to train, throwing weights around for hours and pushing themselves and their bodies to unbelievable lengths.

'As happy as I was when I arrived, especially with my play under a new system, I found life very hard in training. I'm glad I went to rugby league, though. At Kelso I had worked as a roofer and it's safer with both feet on the ground – even in rugby league. Even under a high, hanging kick!'

I'm glad I stuck with the early training regime at Widnes and was not broken before I had even begun. Mind you, at my next club, Leeds, I was to come across a fitness coach who really knew how to push back the barriers. Fortunately, by the time we met I had earned an interesting nickname. They called me 'The Winner'.

Doug Laughton recalls signing me for Widnes:

Ike Southward, sitting up in Workington, must have been prophetic to have phoned me at Widnes around the time I was digesting that paragraph in the *Liverpool Echo* about a young Scottish rugby union international being on the wanted list at St Helens. Ike, who had good relations with the club, told me, 'You don't mind rugby union lads at Widnes, do you? This one's Dad played, and if he's half as tough he'll be all right.' Ike described Alan jnr as a 'marra', which, roughly translated from Cumbrian dialect, means solid and reliable. In terms of recommendation he was off to a flying start.

I had a word with the Widnes committee and off I went on the trail, because not only did Alan seem a decent player with an encouraging pedigree, but I also reckoned I had spotted a gap in the transfer market which ex-union players could help me fill. The door is now shut, of course, but I reckoned I had a fair chance of getting quality for next to nothing compared to what I'd have to pay in league in transfer fees. League players at the time I was signing the likes of Alan Tait were wanting around £20,000 a year plus bonuses. The union lads weren't too aware of the going rate and could be tempted by the prospect of lengthy contracts plus bonus money.

To an extent I was conning the rugby union players by talking about ten-year deals plus other perks. But I also knew that if they were to prove good enough for league I'd bring the deal forward and condense it. There was just no point in getting a player on a bargain and knowing he had the potential to be a good member of the squad if you were going to be sure he would be unhappy or disgruntled.

One thing I had learned was that although you tell players

not to discuss their personal terms, they do talk as soon as they get into each other's company socially. So I worked on the principle I had nothing to lose by offering ten-year deals, because if the player was a success I'd improve his lot in keeping with the others in the squad. On the other hand, I was banking on the fact that nobody wants to hang around if they know things aren't working out and they aren't fitting in. They'll want to get on with the rest of their life.

In Alan's case, he was perhaps a bit too desperate to sign rugby league forms. When I asked him to name his price, he really didn't have much of a clue and said he just wanted to try league. I said, I haven't heard that, Alan. I represent Widnes rugby league club and I'm supposed to get you as cheaply as I can. Now, if you care to mention a figure – and remember, I'm talking a ten-year deal – I'll see what I can do. But, to help you along, if the figure is too high I'll cough, and if the figure is too low I'll rub my nose. I ended up rubbing and coughing until the deal was settled to mutual benefit, because Alan was delighted and I was well inside the figure the Widnes board had given me to play with.

In going after a rugby union player it was mostly a case of backing judgement and following instinct. My motto in all walks of life is 'use your eyes', and it was that same principle that persuaded me to buy a clock in a pub for £250 and sell it on for £600. I had done my homework and knew it was worth more.

As soon as Widnes signed a player we told them to come to the club as soon as they could in the best possible shape. When Alan signed we had a training exercise called 'ten on a bike', which basically meant running from the try-line to the twenty-two ten times. It's called 'the bleep test' nowadays. Ten on a bike was a great exercise because it stretched everybody out side by side, kings and commoners, and there was no hiding place. When Alan first did that exercise he was sick, but within four or five weeks he was leading the pack. A lot of players can do it on the training field but not on the pitch. If you can't do it on the training field, you'll never do it on the pitch. Alan was up with the leaders on both counts, which is why I also signed him for Leeds when I moved on, convinced that if I'd stayed at Widnes I'd have had to sell more quality players than I bought.

A coach can ruin a great side by putting one player in the wrong slot. So, a lot of thought went into playing Taity at full-back, but I reckoned the game needed another dimension. My reasoning was that he would provide bursts of pace from the back and he would appear in gaps and then throw the ball out to Offiah with this remarkable awareness of where the winger was. At times the way that pair linked up was the sporting equivalent of a Van Gogh painting in terms of the admiration it provoked.

When Alan first came to rugby league, though, I didn't really need him. I was planning ahead and stuck him on the wing to begin with because he had pace. He wasn't going to oust either of my centres, but full-back became an optimum berth because it gave Alan more scope to express his abilities.

Teams always need a fast back three. That's where tries are created and Alan was an integral part of my philosophy that pace beats everything. In fact, you can't win without it, and a pass will always beat a running man. That's why I lobbed Alan into a Premiership final even though he'd only had a couple of games as a sub.

The Widnes team that he played in was built on the basis that a pat on the back is more productive than a kick up the arse. Any coach who goes in with a machine-gun approach hasn't a hope in hell. Best to go in wearing slippers. Also, if you let a tradesman stop for a tea interval you'll get a lot more out of him than if he were driven all the time. I'm amazed how many bosses fail to see that, and Alan Tait certainly responded. Mind you, I was probably the only coach who could handle Alan because he was a whinger all the time we worked together. Taity used to whinge about what time the binmen were arriving to empty the bins at the club – but what a perfectionist.

I'll still look out to see how he's doing when I'm 90 years old because he wears his heart on his sleeve. You know exactly where you stand with Alan. He says what he thinks. By contrast, I know people who are upset but still smile. Only trouble is they are sticking a knife in your back at the same time. Taity calls it as he sees it. Some coaches can't handle that, but my view was that if a player had a grievance – legitimate or otherwise – he had to be given a hearing. I'd always say, 'Look, come here, mate. What's the problem?' Having heard what the problem was I'd then have to keep an open mind and make a judgement based on whether it would benefit the team. If it did, it was a case of count me in.

Very seldom was Taity wrong, and he'd even blurt out about players who had gone on the booze if he thought it was affecting the team. Not behind their backs. While they were in the room. By the same token, I have my doubts about Alan making a great coach, and his future in rugby will be more as a fitness consultant/ development officer because he is too open. I kept telling him that in war the great generals didn't lead from the front. Rather they'd be on their white chargers, directing operations from the hill, because to be a coach you have to be a bit smarter than the rest. I'd always be telling Alan, 'You might say what everybody else is thinking. But you get the stick. You don't always need to say what you are thinking.'

I just wish, though, I'd had another ten like Alan Tait under my charge during my time with him at Widnes and Leeds rugby league clubs.

CHAPTER FIVE

Headingley Heaven and Hell

After four years and 136 appearances at Widnes, I felt my rugby league career had started to stagnate. It was time to move on, and there was only one place I really wanted to go by the end of the 1991–92 season – Leeds. Linking up with coach Doug Laughton, who had moved across the Pennines a year earlier, held bags of appeal, not least because it was he who had plucked me out of rugby union.

I'd lost my place in the Great Britain squad for the summer tour of Australasia during my final season at Widnes and it was increasingly obvious that I didn't fit into the club's long-term plans either. I asked Frank Myler, who had succeeded Doug Laughton, if it would be better for me and the club if I hopped on my bike, and within 24 hours I read in the press I'd been transfer-listed for £230,000. The price tag seemed unrealistic, but what really got to me was the suggestion that the club were in some way offended by my offer of a clean break which I thought would be of mutual benefit. Peter Wilkinson, the Widnes secretary, made out that the club were reluctant to put me on the list when, in fact, it seemed to me they'd have been content with a reasonable offer at the end of a season in which I had been beset by hamstring problems.

Doug Laughton knew where my heart lay and that he could trust me to put myself on the line for him. Fortunately his interest was not long being kindled. Any stalemate over the fee, meanwhile, was soon broken by Leeds offering a part-exchange for my services. Bobbie Goulding, a scrum-half who had joined Leeds from Wigan for £90,000 a year earlier, was the player eventually offered, and the move was to prove attractive to him as well in view of the fact that Widnes was his home town.

As I told Martin Richards of the *Daily Mirror*, 'I'm really pleased. I've enjoyed my four years at Widnes but I think a change of clubs will help me get back on the international scene. I hope to be able to use my kicking game at Leeds. It was taken off me at Widnes with Jonathan Davies doing most of the tactical kicking and I've been told it cost me a Great Britain tour chance.'

Ian Proctor also noted in *The Rugby Leaguer* that there was a touch of *déjà vu* about me linking up with Doug Laughton and was also kind enough to state, 'Leeds fans are well aware of Tait's abilities. He scored one of the tries which destroyed them in the Regal Trophy final and two on Widnes's last visit to Headingley.'

That was indeed a reason to be cheerful, but I was just thrilled to be joining a high-profile club, especially one coached by Doug Laughton. In fact my desire to play for Leeds was entirely down to my faith in Doug's ability to put things right, both for me and for a club whom I'd helped Widnes thrash 24–0 the previous season in that Regal Trophy final.

I knew too it was only a matter of time until Doug came in for me provided I maintained form, because we'd kept in touch and I knew he was intent on virtually rebuilding the Leeds team from scratch. Doug told me there were approximately 17 players he wanted to get rid of and confided that before joining Leeds he had gone to see them play Wigan in a match memorable for Martin Offiah scoring ten tries for the red and whites. That was the final match of the season at Leeds, and for any player to get ten tries in the course of 80 minutes is phenomenal. It also showed, however, that there were individuals in the defending team who had knocked off early for the summer break and who in any case were no longer playing for the jersey.

Among the Leeds players that night was John Bentley, later a colleague at Newcastle rugby union club and a fellow British Lion. Doug has told how, in the aftermath of the Wigan débâcle, he actually came across Bentley singing 'Raindrops keep falling on my head', seemingly oblivious to the pain that had been inflicted and pleading in mitigation of himself that he had only come on as a substitute.

So, Doug had virtually all summer to organise a clear-out and eventually came back and signed players from Widnes he knew would give their all for him – myself, Richie Eyres, Harvey Howard and

Esene Faimalo. In addition he snapped up Neil Harmon from War-rington and Jim Fallon from Bath rugby union club. But, whereas I had originally signed for Doug at the tail end of a season, this time round the new campaign was fast approaching. With the team so unsettled it was hardly surprising we needed much of the 1992–93 season to develop some cohesion, but at least the foundations were laid.

It was the following summer that I really derived the benefits from the club's Australian fitness guru, Bob Lannigan, and he was a person with whom I really hit it off straightaway. That was another thing about Leeds – they could afford specialists, whereas at Widnes we had always had to do things on our own. Lannigan had worked with the Australian club Parramatta as well as Wigan and had few peers. He had also worked as a corner-man to champion boxer Terry Fenwick, but what really struck me about his credentials was the fact he had trained the all-conquering Australian Kangaroos rugby league team.

This was the training structure Bob brought to Leeds, and I remember the first day I met him, which was before I had actually played for my new club. I was visiting family in Scotland when Doug phoned and said, 'I want you back. We've got a new fitness coach and he'd like a look at you.' Andy Gregory, the Great Britain scrum-half who was at Leeds, was a good friend of Bob's. As I walked into the Leeds gym for the first time, Andy turned to Bob and said, 'This is the man you'll enjoy training.' I could tell as soon as I shook Bob's hand and looked in his eyes he wanted to test me to my limits. And, knowing the calibre of sportsman he was used to working with, I was determined not to let him down. Everything he asked me to do I completed. With interest.

All the way through our sessions I was driven by the memory of that first day with Widnes, and the humiliation of being sick over the fence had haunted me ever since. Never again, I had vowed, and I was as good as my word. So much so that when Bob left to join coach John Monie at the Auckland Warriors, we had a long conversation in which he complimented me by saying I was one of the top ten guys he had trained in terms of aerobic capacity and sprinting ability. Believe me. These kind of remarks you remember.

The secret of Bob's ability lay in the fact that he developed a regime specific to rugby league players. And, at the end of the day, a rugby player is looking for exercises that will improve his skills in passing, tackling, speed and scrummaging. Strength is mainly in the forearms, back and legs and should be related to ball work. Rugby requires a different kind of speed since we are not endurance athletes. Bob's drills are in tune with those requirements and a lot of the youngsters at Leeds, from what I hear, are still following his doctrines today. For my part, I've learned by adding new drills and by nit-picking, because not everything even acknowledged experts tell you necessarily suits individual requirements. So long as I can say, well, this works for me but that doesn't, that's fine as far as I'm concerned.

That first season at Leeds may not have brought honours for the club but it certainly boosted me to the extent I was drafted into the Great Britain squad as a substitute for the World Cup final against Australia, of which more later. I was also fortunate to be named in the 'form side' of the Stones Bitter Championship, as selected by the leading coaches. In fact, only two players were selected from outside Wigan and St Helens: myself and Castleford loose forward Tawera Nikau. The side read: Alan Tait (Leeds), Alan Hunte (St Helens), Dean Bell (Wigan), Gary Connolly (St Helens), Martin Offiah (Wigan), Tea Ropati (Wigan), Shaun Edwards (Wigan), Kevin Ward (St Helens), Barrie McDermott (Wigan), Andy Platt (Wigan), Denis Betts (Wigan), Phil Clarke (Wigan), Tawera Nikau (Castleford).

Among my regular team-mates at Leeds was Craig Innes, one of two ex-All Blacks at the club, the other being John Gallagher – a different kettle of fish entirely, I'm afraid. John played against me in the 1987 rugby union World Cup and was a thoroughly nice lad. Sure, he had a lot going for him, and nobody can take away his achievement of playing in an All Black World Cup-winning team. But when push came to shove in rugby league, John didn't have the mean streak, and I put it down to the fact he switched codes primarily for money. This is a mistake a lot of players make. Only those prepared to work hard avoid big, big trouble.

I took John Gallagher's place at full-back for Leeds and he hung around for a year before eventually being released and going to London. If John was at his best in an amateur environment, it was a pleasure and a privilege for me to be in the close company at Leeds of someone I had long admired for sheer awe-inspiring professionalism. I refer, of course, to Ellery Hanley.

Doug Laughton inherited the services of Hanley, who gave me a new insight into the conditioning required for top-class rugby. I was also rapt by the competitive way in which he went about achieving that goal. When I arrived at the club Ellery was in his thirties but still leading from the front. In training or on the playing field, this guy's attitude was second to none. I thought, is there some way I can direct my career to being like Ellery? I tuned my approach to his and that wouldn't have been possible without speaking to Ellery a lot.

Contrary to what some might imagine, I had no trouble striking up a dialogue. It's just the media Ellery has a built-in problem with, something to do with the attention that was focused on him after a few scrapes in his youth. Consequently when Ellery found himself in a position of responsibility where he had to speak publicly, the fact that he said anything at all made bigger headlines than the actual content of his remarks. It was bizarre. I don't want to pass judgement on Ellery's taciturn public front, but it is a pity he felt obliged to take such an attitude. He had a tremendous capacity for generating good publicity for the game, had he been willing to share his thoughts more openly.

What I quickly realised from our private discussions was that Ellery Hanley wanted people alongside him who would show the type of commitment he demonstrated, and that meant bodies being put on the line – never a problem as far as I was concerned.

In emulating Ellery I had also committed myself to a long summer of training, because my role model was very much his own man and did things his way. What makes training far more enjoyable, of course, is having somebody to measure yourself against, and I was lucky to be at the same club as Hanley. From the start Ellery spotted something in me that he could use, and mutual benefits quickly accrued. When I arrived at Leeds we knew each other from the Great Britain team but he wanted to find me out as a trainer. In rugby league training it is not advisable to concentrate on one aspect of fitness; you should instead do a lot of weights, endurance and sprint work. It can be either a mile slog or a five-yard sprint, and I am proud to say it was Hanley who nicknamed me 'The Winner'. That label is something to which I attach the highest regard, and it was bestowed by Ellery because he could never get the better of me overall. If there was a challenge on the table, though, I would get butterflies in the stomach because I knew I would be the yardstick for everyone else.

Ellery used to wind me up, and out of deference to the prize bestowed on the leader of the Tour de France cycle race we would even have our own yellow jersey to signify who had the edge in training. Competition was all very light-hearted. But there was an edge, too, which we both used to our advantage, and all the time the youngsters – Leeds signed some good ones – were looking at me to set the standard either in the gym or on the track.

The experience taught me that, as Scottish rugby union continues to go through a turbulent phase with the transition to professionalism, things must eventually settle down with each club having a figurehead for every aspirant to look up to and whose methods can be copied. It helped all the big clubs in rugby league to have that sort of individual and at Widnes I was lucky to have the perfect role model in Kurt Sorensen. When I arrived Kurt was well into his thirties, but he looked after himself so well. A virtual tee-totaller, Kurt always led from the front and after every home game would nip away for a 15-minute cold bath before returning for something to eat and drink. That's the kind of professional Kurt was: somebody getting near the end of his career and doing everything possible to extend his shelf life. I'm at that stage now myself and hopefully the lessons taught by players like Ellery and Kurt have rubbed off.

We really needed to be fit at Leeds, too, because, like Manchester United in football, everybody wanted to claim our scalp. That was one difference I found straightaway on pitching up from Naughton Park, Widnes. There, success seemed to be a bonus. At Leeds it was expected, and as soon as I arrived I was aware of fans asking when the trophies would start accumulating. I also quickly noticed that if, for example, Featherstone Rovers went two tries behind against Widnes, you instinctively knew it would turn into a rout. But, against Leeds, who were a monied club, the opposition were going to try twice as hard. Doug Laughton knew when he moved what he was up against in terms of sheer weight of expectation and made a habit of signing players with a lot of bottle.

It was with Leeds in 1994 that I finally achieved my dream of winning through to a Wembley Challenge Cup final. I was beginning to think I'd never make it – the previous year in the semi Leeds had been beaten by, irony of ironies, Widnes – when another opportunity arose. That Widnes defeat, by the crushing margin of 39–4, was, as you might expect, a hammer blow, and I'll never forget Doug Laughton's face after the game. We looked at each other in stunned disbelief. The team he had created and the one I'd been so much a part of had made it to Wembley – and neither Doug nor I was going with them. At least Doug had been to Wembley as a player with Wigan, but there were no guarantees I'd ever make that long walk up the tunnel before plunging into an ocean of colour.

We drew St Helens in the '94 semi and amidst emotional scenes at Central Park I snaffled 'man of the match' in a 20–8 victory despite the fact that Ellery Hanley grabbed two tries. Leeds were on their way to Wembley for the first time in 16 years and on the way home, still in a frenzied excitement, I called my Dad on a mobile phone. My Dad was always brilliant at keeping my feet on the ground but on this occasion he surpassed himself. I remember his words clearly after I'd informed him we'd just made it to every rugby league fan's Mecca. 'Well,' he replied, 'your forwards are going to have to play better than that.'

Later, and despite parental counsel not to get carried away, I was gushing in praise of Hanley in the *Daily Mirror*, where I told Martin Richards, 'The man is a legend. His tackling and support play were outstanding and I'm pleased for him we're going to Wembley.'

Truth to tell I was rapturous to be going to play beneath the twin towers for myself. When I was a boy my Dad would always go to Wembley, usually in the Workington Town club bus. And, after every trip, Dad would bring me back a souvenir, normally a rosette, which I'd pin to my wardrobe. I think, too, watching me in a Challenge Cup final might have represented a pinnacle for my Dad, especially as when I played with Kelso he struggled to get along to Poynder Park, a mile or so down the road from home. Wembley, though, was different. Dad would have walked there on Challenge Cup final day – irrespective of who was playing – if he'd had to.

The first time I watched a Challenge Cup final on television, I set my heart on playing on that magnificent stage where supporters of all clubs gather to create a family atmosphere that reflects nothing but credit on the sport and on all concerned. The trouble was that Leeds could never get the measure of Wigan, twice our conquerors, on the big occasion. Wigan were absolutely awesome in making it seven wins in a row after a match memorable for one of the greatest tries in the 65-year history of Wembley, the first of two scored by Martin Offiah. Unfortunately I had a central role in taking on the impossible and trying to defend against Martin's blistering pace. I do, however, earn a mention in Martin's autobiography, *Fast and Loose*, in which he describes the try, saying,

If someone asked me to pick out just one try that sums up what I'm about, then I'd have to pick the one against Leeds at Wembley in 1994: it had everything.

The try was something really special, though I'm sure you need a fair amount of luck to score a try like that on such a big occasion. As a winger, you dream about getting the ball under your own posts and running the length of the field to score, but to do it in front of 80,000 people in the Challenge Cup final, with millions watching on television round the world, well, it doesn't get any better than that for a rugby league player.

The opening 14 minutes had been quite tough, with Leeds putting Wigan under a considerable amount of pressure that we had to soak up. On one of their attacks a kick was put through to our posts and Gary Connolly, who was playing full-back, gathered it and took the tackle. Frano Botica went to dummy-half and I came in quite late off the left wing to take his pass before moving down the right. My idea had been just to make as many yards as possible, but suddenly a gap seemed to open up and I went for it. I remember stepping outside Neil Harmon, the Leeds prop, and then I had broken through the Leeds defensive line. Now I was in open space and coming up to the halfway line.

In situations like this you don't really think about scoring, but just about making as much ground as possible. I knew that I wouldn't be caught from behind once I was into open space, because no matter how quick someone is it's hard for them to turn and catch you once you've gone past them. The only player between me and the try-line was Alan Tait, their full-back and my old team-mate from Widnes – so now it was a battle between him and me, and I knew he was pretty quick. I didn't really know what I was going to do, but I think that instinct takes over at times like this.

Normally Alan's one of those players who shows an opponent the outside and uses his speed to cut them down. But this time I had the whole field to play with, so I had the initiative. I decided to keep him guessing as to which way I was going to go, so I angled my run to take him left first and then right – before accelerating for the line. That meant he would have to chase me, and I knew that he couldn't catch me.

The next time I came up against Alan was in 1997, when we were both playing rugby union – he was with Newcastle and I was playing for Bedford. I had a chat to him after the game and I told him that any time I felt bad I watched that try on video and it cheered me up. I pointed out that it had made him famous.

My recollection of one of the great Wembley tries was that Martin was the only player who could have left me for dead in a sprint, and I reckon he would have been Olympic class had he geared his sporting career that way. As Martin broke clear that day there was only me blocking the way to the goal-line, and I tried to draw him on to me while signalling to colleague Francis Cummins to cover round behind me. Alas, Francis had given up the ghost and I'll always wonder if I could have got to Martin in a straight dash for the corner.

After being drawn infield, Martin, who was awarded the Lance Todd Trophy for man of the match, suddenly took off and moment-arily I slipped. In the circumstances I suppose I did a half-decent job in pushing him out near the corner so that Frano Botica missed the conversion. I gave him the outside, as a full-back is supposed to do, and if I was a part of something special then all well and good. Martin was truly a phenomenon who, in his début season at Widnes, scored 45 tries. They said, incidentally, that that total would never be beaten, but in the first year I played with him at Widnes he got 60 and, in all honesty, I must have laid on a third of them.

During my union career I had been criticised for holding up the ball after going through a gap, but linking with Offiah eliminated that tendency. My Dad once had an interesting discussion on that subject with Johnny Gray, a former South of Scotland rugby union coach, when they met by chance at the Skittle Bar in Kelso. South had just played the Anglos at Hawick and Johnny reckoned I could have done more damage had I not hung around looking for support after breaking the initial tackle. I knew that some of the others in the South three-quarter line couldn't keep pace, but with Offiah there was no such problem.

I was sorry when Martin and I went our different ways, but at Leeds I came into contact with a different kind of try-scoring phenomenon in that man Ellery Hanley. Known as 'The Poacher', Hanley was virtually always offside but invariably got away with it. He had a knack of waiting until the ball was kicked down to me at full-back and instead of retreating like the rest of the team managed to linger in no-man's land. That way Ellery knew he could slip in behind me as I ran the ball upfield and tries would be up for grabs. Commentators who had, naturally, been following the ball would wonder what sort of trap-door Ellery had slipped out of, but we had things in perfect synch. It was an example of players reading each other's games, and in contrasting fashion I struck it off with Ellery just as well as I had done with Martin before he moved on to Wigan in a British record deal of £440,000.

It was a shame Ellery and I couldn't manufacture enough chances on our big day at Wembley when we went down 26–16, and without making excuses maybe it had something to do with the fact that he'd been forced to seek specialist treatment in Hawick from local osteopath Harry Whittaker for a hamstring problem. Harry's the best in the business in my book and succeeded in getting Ellery on the pitch when the general prognosis was he wouldn't make it. But the fitness battle had maybe taken its toll. To be blunt, I think he was still carrying that injury despite Harry's best efforts.

There was an up side for the Leeds captain, though. On his trip to the Borders, Harry Whittaker would take him for walks over the hills and it seemed to strike a chord with Ellery that the lambs had a tough life being bothered by foxes so frequently. For weeks afterwards he would tell me, 'These young lambs don't half have it tough up in Hawick.' For Ellery the city dweller, his quest for fitness had provided a culture shock as well!

Leeds were to qualify for another trip to Wembley the following year after a marvellous semi-final with Featherstone Rovers at Elland

Road, home of Leeds United football club. There must be days when professional golfers stand over a putt and know they can't miss, or when basketball players net every time with three-point throws. It's my experience that rugby can be a bit like that. In fact, there are times when a player feels he can even control the bounce of the ball by will-power alone. One such occasion was that Featherstone Rovers tie, probably the finest game of rugby I've played in my life.

The omens were certainly good because it was the type of surface I always pray for – short grass on a wide pitch. I scored a long-range try, managed to involve myself in every move, and picked up the man-of-the-match award in our 39–22 victory. It was just one of those games. Whether the ball bounced right or left, I was usually there waiting to run on to it. Everything fell into place after a shaky start, and in helping the team to the Challenge Cup final at Wembley for the second time in my career I felt I never made a mistake. Doug Laughton was later heard to claim that he had predicted to Leeds officials that the occasion and the surroundings would be tailor-made for me. Apparently a club official had been told not to worry and that 'Taity will cut 'em to ribbons'. I'm glad I didn't prove a disappointment in a match which gave Featherstone the dubious consolation of scoring more points than any other beaten Challenge Cup semi-finalists, a record set by Oldham the previous year.

Once again our final rivals were to be Wigan, and as I looked forward to Wembley by claiming we had simply got ourselves too hyped up against them a year earlier and that we would be more settled this time, little did I know that massive upheaval for the game and desperate family difficulties for Caroline and me were lurking just around the corner.

Spring of 1995 saw the first shots fired in an amazing battle for the heart, soul . . . and commercial rights to rugby league. Initially the battleground was 'down under', where the Australian Rugby League had a deal with media mogul Kerry Packer giving him the rights to show the sport on his Channel Nine broadcasting station. Just to give an example of how big rugby league is in Australia, I remember hearing how, when the Scottish rugby union team played a Test match with the world champion Wallabies at Sydney Football Stadium in 1992, it was a club rugby league match which attracted live radio coverage that day, with mere score updates from the international encounter!

Frustrated at being denied access to such a massive sport and its audiences, Packer's rival Rupert Murdoch hatched a scheme to start an alternative competition, to be known as 'Super League'. Murdoch's grand plan saw him sign not just players but well-known clubs such as Brisbane Broncos, Canberra Raiders and Auckland Warriors. It was a case of why stop there, though, as far as the Murdoch people were concerned. The next stage in their plan called for Super League to become established in Europe, with a regular trans-hemisphere competition which would help make rugby league into a global game, bearing in mind Murdoch has massive television interests in Asia keen to show live sporting action. If rugby union had the international scene sewn up, then the alternative, as far as Murdoch was concerned, was to go down the club route.

European Super League won the approval of the British bosses of rugby league's governing body, but the ARL weren't to take things lying down and set about a spoiling operation based on trying to sign the best players here for clubs over in Australia in order to thwart the Murdoch plan. Talk about a seller's market so far as players were concerned – and I was in the middle of it! The trouble was that everything erupted during the build-up to Wembley, when we should have had other matters on our minds.

What rankled with many Leeds players was a suspicion that special payments to stay loyal to Super League were being channelled first and foremost in the direction of our Wigan opponents. While the Wigan players' futures were secure, over at poor relations Leeds many individuals were facing massive uncertainty, not knowing whether they were in line for Super League money and, if they were, how much. There were also divisions arising from the fact that some – but not all – were being head-hunted by the Australian Rugby League.

As a background to all this, there was uproar when it emerged that in order to raise standards many renowned British clubs were to be amalgamated. And, of course, the season was to switch to summer in synch with the southern hemisphere – something that horrified me, not least because I have an aversion to hard grounds.

Maurice Lindsay, Chief Executive of the Rugby League, wanted smaller clubs such as Featherstone and Castleford to merge and play in new stadiums to raise the standard and the image of the sport.

Widnes were another side expected to amalgamate, and my heart went out to their fans who were unbelievably unfortunate, having seen their team nearly always finish in the top three in the period just before the advent of Super League.

The Widnes team started to break up immediately before Super League reared its head, and so this great club was to be left out in the cold. Thousands of people turned up at games to demonstrate rather than to watch the rugby, and the revolt upset a lot of players. Everything happened so very, very fast. In retrospect, I know a lot of these decisions had to be made. But they were harsh ones and the Widnes supporters must have been devastated, as must the players and the coaches.

New rules were to be introduced, but the biggest change of all would be moving rugby league in Britain to the summer. Players who had just finished a hard season simply had to be ready to start up again. Summer rugby didn't really appeal to me because it made the days long and boring, quite apart from the hard going underfoot. I faced the prospect of sitting in the house all day, keeping out of the sun, to play at night.

A lot didn't seem fair at the time, but Super League has now been proved to be the right course. In rugby league nowadays backs are still against the wall, but it remains a great game to watch and now has more exposure, which is benefiting the players, who are now better off. There are signs too of Super League expanding, with an imaginative 'on the road' scheme which takes teams into uncharted territory to play meaningful matches with championship points at stake. There's even talk of a franchise for either Edinburgh or Glasgow, which will be a major blow to rugby union if it doesn't get its act together and iron out a series of squabbles mainly involving clubs and the governing body.

There can be no denying that at the time Super League was being set up some players were being made offers it was hard to refuse, myself included, although I was to be reminded in the middle of all the negotiations that health is something money can't buy. Rugby league politics caught up with me when, out of the blue, my agent, Dave McKnight of the sports management firm Premier Crew, telephoned and told me to get to a Bradford hotel straightaway because the two organisations were fighting over the signatures of players. My contract with Leeds expired at the end of the season and so I had absolutely nothing to lose by driving to Bradford. Actually Doug Laughton had cautioned against rushing into any new deal with the club because if the team got to Wembley there would be more money in the pot, and it left me in an exciting negotiating position.

My ship had come in, it seemed, with that call telling me to head for Bradford, where I found a room full of top players, including the Wigan trio of Andy Farrell, Kelvin Skerrett and Jason Robinson, ready to talk to the ARL. Ellery Hanley, also a household name in rugby league and a Leeds colleague, was there too but – typically – he seemed to be operating from a different agenda. Indeed, Ellery was in a different room from the others, who were checking by mobile phone to see what terms were likely to be offered by Super League. The players were playing one group off against the other – and we were not talking pennies, either. Rather thousands of pounds.

Before leaving for Bradford I had told Caroline I wouldn't sign without talking to her because, obviously, if you agree to play in Australia you have to go and live there, which is an upheaval by anyone's standards! But I knew I was playing the best rugby league of my life and that the timing of the discussions was perfect. Nevertheless, I was resolved not to sign when the ARL representative called me into the room, ticked my name off and asked if I knew any of their clubs. I had agreed twice previously in my career to join North Sydney Bears, but on both occasions I had got injured and had to pull out. Naturally I mentioned the Bears, and he said it wouldn't be a problem if I fancied playing for them and pledged they would come up with a contract once I had signed for the ARL in the ploy calculated to spoil the Super League plans.

Having established that the contract was to commit myself to the ARL and not to Super League, I asked what sort of money was being offered. The response was along the lines of £100,000 to sign on there and then, plus £75,000 for each of two subsequent years. Now, I regarded myself as an experienced professional and proved it by resisting – just – the temptation to throw my hands in the air, cheer and run round the room. Somehow I managed to fix an expression which suggested I was really considering the offer and not one which betrayed true feelings, namely that I couldn't believe my good luck. After all, at Leeds I was receiving half that amount.

I said I wanted a word with my agent in private and asked him what he expected as a cut. Dave McKnight had always been fair with me and we agreed that our normal arrangement of a down payment rather than a percentage would apply. That down payment was to be £7,500, and we shook hands. Certainly Dave was under the impression I was about to go back into the room to agree the offer. So, you could have knocked him down with a feather when I told the ARL rep, 'You've got a deal if you knock the offer up to £100,000 in each of the three years.' The ARL rep agreed on the spot and Dave gave me a look which said 'You cheeky blighter!'.

There I was, then, with £300,000 mine for the taking, but first I had to speak to Doug Laughton, which was easier said than done. I tried everywhere, from his home to the rugby club. I even told Doug's wife, Joan, about the money I was finding hard to refuse. I needed to know what Doug's contract offer at Leeds would be – it was only courtesy – but I couldn't get through to him to find out what was going on. Wigan's players certainly knew what was going on and it only seemed to be them who were in with a shout of the big-money deals from Super League.

I asked the ARL guy for half an hour's grace, but when he couldn't give me any longer I went into the room and signed. Driving back to Leeds I kept having to pinch myself, because there I was, committed to a new life in Australia and with a Wembley cup final looming. I drove straight to Doug Laughton's house and, after explaining what I'd done, heard him becoming increasingly upset. It emerged that the ARL hadn't approached just me but also three other Leeds players – Kevin Iro, Craig Innes and Ellery Hanley – which meant that the team Doug Laughton had built was being destroyed at a stroke. Wigan, allegedly, had all their players tied up on Super League contracts but Leeds were split, even though Doug did eventually manage to persuade Kevin Iro to remain at Headingley.

Leeds went to Wembley in 1995 with half the players shouting for Super League loyalty money they had never been offered, which was not the best way to approach a Challenge Cup final. The Wigan guys, on the other hand, were being linked with a £20,000 virtual bonus for staying put at Central Park and were going down Wembley Way a thoroughly contented bunch. By contrast, Leeds were tearing each other limb from limb, knowing one of their number had netted a cool

£300,000 but there was nobody for the majority of the others to talk to. At the end of the day we were well beaten 30–10 and I put it down to the money causing disharmony in the Leeds camp.

At the post-final dinner Doug Laughton made a speech in which he came close to saying good riddance to me, Ellery Hanley and Craig Innes. That upset me, partly because I regarded Doug as a friend who had to realise I did what was best for my family, but also because my Mum, sister and wife were present at the function. It wasn't the time or the place to uncork frustration, but I also knew the pressure Doug was under. Super League had sorted out Wigan but not Leeds – or so it seemed – and Doug had suffered as a consequence.

While the ructions over Super League and the ARL signings were rumbling on, though, I was experiencing the worst times of my life off the field. My son, Mike, had gone to hospital for a scan for what we thought was a bladder infection. In fact, the doctor said the scan showed a black shape which had to be examined more closely. With me preoccupied by the impending move to Australia, it was left to Caroline to ferry Mike backwards and forwards to hospital for the tests we were sure would turn out to show an easily treatable infection. Eventually we got a letter telling us to take Mike to the oncology unit at St James's Hospital in Leeds – and that's when the penny dropped. Suddenly we realised that Mike's condition had to be cancer-related, and I downed tools on rugby 100 per cent. In fact, my whole life suddenly ground to a halt as I found myself staring into an abyss and pondering the sheer nonsense of those oft-repeated remarks about sport being more important than life or death.

While our families back in the Borders still believed Mike was suffering from an infection, Caroline and I sat in a hospital room awaiting the doctor's verdict. Full marks to St James's – or St Jimmy's, as it is affectionately referred to in Leeds – whose medical staff didn't beat about the bush. I suppose that was understandable, but, anyway, the doctor came in and got straight to the point. I'll never forget the following numbing words: 'I have to tell you exactly what is going on. Michael has a tumour on his adrenalin gland which needs to be removed straightaway. If the tumour is benign he'll just have tests until it's cleared up. If, however, the tumour is malignant he'll start radiotherapy and chemotherapy almost immediately.'

These revelations left me devastated. My life was now in turmoil and things were coming at me from all angles – although rugby league suddenly didn't matter a jot. The worst bit of all was phoning my parents, because Caroline was too upset to call and left the task to me. In fact, I quickly realised I couldn't speak either, having succumbed to emotion, and as the phone line clicked dead in mid-conversation my Mum was left wondering what on earth was going on. Eventually Caroline pulled herself together long enough to explain to our families in the briefest of terms the specialist's diagnosis.

The shock didn't really hit us until we went back home and shut the front door. Michael was still at school, enjoying life and blissfully unaware of his condition. After about an hour I composed myself well enough to have conversations with the folks back home. Both my Mum and Caroline's Mum headed south to lend support, knowing that Mike would be in hospital for four or five days. In fact, a major operation had to be performed on young Mike in which surgeons removed his stomach from the back to find – thankfully – a benign tumour. Further checks showed that only three people in a million get that form of cancer and it had to be ascertained whether it was hereditary. The experience made me wonder, too, whether we are all carrying something like this.

Mike's subsequent all-clear was a huge weight off my shoulders, but I still had to sort out my contract with the ARL, having come to a decision that I didn't want to remove my youngster who had just had cancer surgery to Australia, where his grandparents wouldn't see him for a long time. I told all this to the ARL, who were very under-standing but pointed out that I had lost a fair amount of cash. I guess the North Sydney Bears and I are destined never to team up, although I truly hesitate to say never after the twists and turns my career has taken! Doug Laughton was also marvellous in helping me hatch a deal with Super League, from whom I received half as much as I would have done from the ARL. But that was just fine, considering I didn't have to leave home.

Two weeks after things were sorted, Doug Laughton left Leeds. His departure marked the beginning of the end of my association with a club he'd always had to battle to hold together on the playing side because of the many factions. Ellery Hanley, while undoubt-edly a great player, wasn't universally popular at Leeds, and dressing-room power struggles which contributed to the break-up of the team also centred on Andy Gregory and Gary Schofield. It seemed to me that Schoey didn't like Ellery and vice versa, while Andy Gregory had his own little clique who liked a few beers together on a Sunday night.

Doug Laughton was usually to be found in the middle trying to calm things down, and it was all very petty, really, especially as everybody was on good wages. Andy stopped talking to me and a few others because we backed Hanley up. As for Schoey, he used to frustrate me as a player because if he hadn't been so caught up in dressing-room politics he could have been even better. And that's saying something. If Schoey wanted to play he could be world class and capable of beating any defence. But on other occasions he would be so erratic. I knew that week in, week out Ellery was the man to be relied upon, so I aligned myself with him. Matters were at their absolute worst approaching that 1993 Challenge Cup semi-final defeat by Widnes which cut me to the quick. I felt that Schofield had taken the huff during the build-up and wasn't properly focused, and that was at the root of the problems.

When Doug Laughton left Headingley, the Leeds committee went for Dean Bell, the former Wigan centre, as coach, with Hugh McGahan as his assistant. The appointments were to mark one of the worst periods in my rugby career – in either code – and not just because I had been Laughton's blue-eyed boy. When the new pair arrived I tried to tell them of my difficult personal circumstances stemming from my son's medical condition; of how I was physically and emotionally drained and that I could hardly lift a dumbbell. But I don't think I got through to them. They were only interested in guys who could do the business on the pitch in the short term.

Both were New Zealanders and tough players in their day. Dean, now 36, compiled an astonishing 27 winners' medals in the British game, while Hugh, also 36, was decorated with the MBE, back in 1991, for services to sport in New Zealand, a country he captained 17 times. Three years earlier he had been awarded the Adidas Golden Boot as the world's finest player. So, they knew their way around. I believed, however, that they should have been a little more sympathetic to my personal circumstances.

One day I received a call to go to Dean's office, where he told me I was not part of his plans. 'I want you to go now' were the words which ensured my Leeds career was on borrowed time. However, I was not prepared to roll over and insisted on receiving what I felt I was due. I said, 'If you pay up, I'll go,' suspecting that they couldn't afford to give me the money still due to me from the Super League contract as a loyalty bonus. It was a case of hanging in there, and as long as I did what I was told on the training field, they couldn't fine me or cancel my contract.

For a year I virtually did no more than turn up to train while Dean Bell kept putting me in the team and then dropping me. He even made me play for the reserves one Christmas Eve against Wigan seconds. I got three tries. I went from playing 37 matches for the club in season 1994–95 to a mere 13 plus three as substitute in 1995–96, as any respect I had for Dean Bell evaporated. Punters might have come to the conclusion I was a fading star. Fair enough. I could understand them forming that impression. What was clear was that I just couldn't perform for Dean Bell on the pitch, and that's a big thing as far as a coach is concerned. If players can't give a coach respect he is in trouble, and Dean Bell had none from me – or, for that matter, from six or seven other players who he mistakenly thought would 'die for him'.

Once Doug Laughton's team started to disperse, it was downhill fast for Leeds. What sustained me as I hung in under Bell's governance was the fact I got on well with the Leeds board of directors. That changed when Gary Hetherington took over as Chief Executive, and because of his support for the new regime I became resigned to moving back to Scotland and the house my Dad had built for us before looking for a nine-to-five job. Normality loomed!

Then, suddenly, rugby union decided to go professional. It could not have happened at a better time as far as I was concerned. I knew instantly I had to get myself fully fit, but that was easier said than done because I had just had an operation on my big toe. The op was, in fact, pre-planned, although Leeds didn't know that at the time. I had a toe that was full of arthritis which I intended having sorted as soon as I retired. But, in the interim, I had met a specialist from Rochdale by the name of Louis Stoddart who was prepared to make me a new joint. That involved three or four months off, and the original intention was to have the break during the winter close season. I hatched a plan to have the op so that I missed a chunk of

Super League – mainly to sicken Dean Bell even more because he had been putting me through hell.

One match day I decided to go down injured in order to come off, saying my toe was in agony. The pain wasn't that acute (I had grown used to pain over four years) and I could have played on. But Dean thought my problem was an in-growing toenail, and he must have got a shock on being told I was out for months. In fact, I heard he asked the club physio for an update on my injury and almost fell off his chair on being told I was sidelined for so long.

It was during this period out injured that I started talking to Newcastle Falcons rugby union team as a prelude to a new and exciting phase in my rugby career. I dread to think, though, about the fact that I could so easily have finished my rugby-playing career at Leeds. I'd have been bitter for the rest of my days. Fortunately I managed to move on to bigger and better things, and neither Dean nor Hugh can take away what I have achieved in the years since I left them.

It's not a nice experience to be told you are not wanted at a club, and the harsh world of professional sport was brought back to me at the beginning of 1998 when the Scottish Rugby Union announced they were cutting their four district teams to two. This came despite players being encouraged to give up their jobs on the back of pledges that the four district teams would run for at least five years. I was at Kelso races when the news broke and I really felt for guys like Scott Welsh, the Hawick and Scotland A stand-off, who was also at the track and who faced a period of uncertainty, although ultimately he was kept on in the new set-up.

Most of the players had given up jobs because of the lure of international rugby, and I know just how strong that can be. During my latter days at Leeds I was invited to captain a Scottish rugby league team against Ireland at the home of Partick Thistle FC. While I regarded myself as flying the flag for the 13-a-side code, the Leeds coaches decided I should be fined for missing a reserve match. It was the final straw. Leeds and I were finished. But how disappointing that I left Leeds without any farewell to the fans who had always given me plenty of encouragement, or a final game in the company of some great players who had also been terrific friends.

When I went to Headingley to negotiate my release, my bags were already packed in the rear of the car ready for a quick getaway to Scotland. In fact, I was well up the A1 before it dawned on me that I had pulled on the Leeds jersey for the last time. Leaving should never be like that, and what a contrast it was to the dignified way in which I was to part company with my next club, Newcastle Falcons.

CHAPTER SIX

Tait on the Tyne

At the start of Newcastle-upon-Tyne's biggest sporting weekend in years, a distraught fan turned in desperation to a *Sky Television* football phone-in programme for urgent assistance.

'It's about my wife,' said the caller. 'She's run off with my best friend.'

On the studio couch, two presenters exchanged nervous glances.

'Er, this isn't the *Jerry Springer Show*, caller,' remarked one of the hosts, in a reference to American TV's top outlet for true-life confessions.

The caller bravely battled on in a bid to be understood, saying, 'No, no. I can live with her leaving me. It's just that she took with her my cup final ticket and I'm running out of time to retrieve it and get to the game.'

The fan supported Newcastle United, who a few hours later were due to challenge Arsenal at Wembley, and his plight aptly summed up what football in particular means to the city.

When I learned of such fanaticism I squirmed with embarrassment because I had the offer of a coveted match ticket guaranteed – and turned it down flat. In normal circumstances, this former Cumbria Schools Under-13 right-back would have jumped at the chance of a football day out at Wembley. But the offer of a ticket came from my Newcastle Falcons rugby union club and just under 24 hours later I was hoping to play a part in helping clinch the Allied Dunbar English Division One title at the first time of asking. Not everybody in the squad felt, as I did, that to go to the cup final ahead of our vital win-or-bust showdown with Harlequins across London at Stoop Memorial Ground wasn't sensible. Far better, I reckoned, to get

Where it all began: Victoria Primary School Under-11 rugby league side. I'm two from the left in the front row, wearing a striped jersey and balancing a ball on my head! I believe that the simpler format of league, compared with union, gets youngsters more accustomed to handling the ball.

The mighty Moor Close Secondary rugby union team from Workington – pride of Cumbria. I'm seated in the centre of the group to the right of skipper Glen Burgess and alongside the curly-headed Ian Bower, both of whom went on to play professional rugby league with their local team.

You can tell which one is me in this Kelso High School rugby union 1st XV group by the pristine condition of my boots, which my mum always insisted I keep well polished. Perhaps that went into the making of a rugby professional!

My big break was undoubtedly being invited to play in a charity rugby union match at Hawick in the mid-1980s for a side selected by Jim Renwick, then Scotland's most capped player. It didn't do much harm either for another up-and-coming youngster by the name of Gavin Hastings, who is in the back row (second left).

Pride of the Borders: a successful season for the South of Scotland rugby union squad was marked by a reception. I'm kneeling two from the left, between Kelso clubmates Sandy Thomson and Roger Baird. Colin Deans, Gordon Hunter and Keith Robertson complete the front-row line-up. Note a youthful-looking Jim Telfer seated on the right of the middle row.

A familiar sight in Scottish rugby union: Kelso displaying a seven-a-side trophy. On this occasion it is the Jed-Forest Cup, just before I left for rugby league.

Catch me if you can: in my other sporting life I competed on the professional sprint circuit and occasionally enjoyed some success.

ABOVE LEFT: Colin 'Charlie' Wright, retired headmaster of Moor Close Secondary, Workington, and a big influence on my early rugby career. ABOVE RIGHT: Ike Southward, the former Great Britain winger and the first player to be transferred for a five-figure sum, played a behind-the-scenes role in my move from Kelso to Widnes.

If the cap fits . . . there's always someone ready to oblige for a silly snap-shot. On the way home from the 1987 Rugby Union World Cup in New Zealand, the Scotland squad dropped in on Disneyland, where Mickey Mouse and his mates must have had a great laugh at our expense.

Celebrating one of Widnes's many trophy successes with Martin Offiah, the fastest player in rugby – union or league (© Sig Kasatkin).

LEFT: If you thought the headgear chosen in Disneyland was off the wall, this is me going native in Papua New Guinea during a Great Britain rugby league tour three years later. Clearly my taste in clothes did not improve with age!

BELOW: With the Great Britain rugby league team which won the second Test against Papua New Guinea in Port Moresby during the 1990 tour.

With Tom Mitchell, a real character of rugby league who, in his capacity as Workington Town chairman, mounted some audacious raids on amateur rugby union in a bid to sign star names.

The Laughton lads. Dougie Laughton (centre) was more than a coach to me in rugby league; he was also a friend and a father figure. I was happy to follow him to Leeds from Widnes along with Richie Eyres (left) and Harvey Howard (© Dave Williams).

to our hotel, put the feet up and watch on the box, especially as I had been to Wembley on rugby league Challenge Cup final duty with Leeds and also with the Scottish rugby union team and knew the congestion fans had to overcome on leaving the stadium.

In fact, I made my feelings known – and maybe a bit too loudly, because when our team for that deciding match at Quins was announced after the rest of the squad returned from the twin towers, I found myself relegated to the substitutes' bench. On reflection, I doubt very much whether my unerring capacity for sounding off when I thought the situation merited such a reaction was a factor influencing coach Steve Bates and director of rugby Rob Andrew in their final team selection. Nevertheless, I did suspect Rob's patience with me was wearing a bit thin. I had, after all, been a critic of the way the Falcons had tightened up during the run-in and were attempting to grind their way to the title through heavy reliance on ten-man rugby. It wouldn't have been that surprising, the thought occurred to me, if I were being taught a lesson for introducing a discordant note.

What I do know is that at around 2.30 p.m. on the Sunday following Newcastle United's 2–0 defeat by Arsenal, the Falcons team were gathered in a huddle awaiting a late conversion which would bring the curtain down on our 44–20 victory. In the middle of that close-knit gathering – I had come on as a second-half substitute for Va'aiga Tuigamala – I was picking my words carefully and drawing heavily on the Ian McGeechan book of logic. Repeating the advice handed out by master coach Geech in the wake of the British Lions Test series triumph in South Africa, I put on my most statesmanlike voice and declared, 'Never forget this moment, because in ten or twenty years' time we could meet up again. It could be in a pub or walking down the street. But we will want to relive the next few seconds over and over again in each other's company.'

It was an intensely emotional gathering which took place moments later when the final whistle sounded, and I was glad we had called time-out to take stock in advance of what we would be celebrating. Newcastle had achieved what many had considered was way beyond us nine months earlier at the beginning of the season, including those bookmakers who had quoted us at 12–1 for the title. What's more, we had gone where no one in England had gone before by becoming the first team to be crowned champions in their first season after gaining promotion.

Newcastle were only the fourth side to win the English League title after Bath, Leicester and Wasps, a feat all the more remarkable considering 28 months earlier we had been languishing at the foot of the Second Division. Sure, there had been rugby success before in the North-East of England, most recently when the Gosforth club captured the John Player Cup in 1977. But that was in a bygone era long before club owner Sir John Hall, surveyor turned speculator, reached for his cheque book and sparked a rugby revolution. How they sneered at Sir John when he embarked on buying a team, claiming that only football and not rugby could sustain such a market. Sir John had proved the doubters wrong in that he could now draw crowds in a rugby backwater and his team had turned the established order on its head.

There was much to celebrate and I had to admit to having been churlish in proclaiming the means by which we finished the season, grinding out wins, unedifying. I had been motivated purely by a desire to be more involved in the proceedings and to exert a greater influence. I had become frustrated when orders were given to kick for position or to play to our gargantuan set of forwards. I had even screamed my head off at Rob Andrew and the skipper, Dean Ryan, and probably upset them a bit. That old failing of not being able to keep my mouth shut. I so much wanted to be part of the victory charge, to win the game with ball in hand. But there was no denying that the tactics worked, and I was as proud as punch of what was indeed a great effort. Once we had embarked on the tactics for the final push and found them to work in home wins over Bristol, Leicester and Bath, why change?

I don't think Tim Stimpson, our Lions full-back, did himself any favours by criticising the approach. Tim, now at Leicester, was out of the team in the second half of the season and it came across that he had an axe to grind. As they always said in Wigan when I was confronted by that incredible machine during my rugby league days, 'If it ain't broke, why fix it?' I had no problem with our restricted approach once the league was won. You don't throw water at somebody who is on a ladder above you. As somebody said, 'How many professional golfers do you see shooting for the pin as opposed to laying up short when they are in the final round of a tournament cushioned by a two- or three-shot lead?' We were in a position where pragmatism had to prevail over cavalier spirit. But sometimes in the front line, with the heart ruling the head, it is damned difficult to accept playing conservatively and chiselling out results.

Alan Hedley, reporter for the *Newcastle Journal* who sportingly honoured a pledge made early in the season to have his head and beard shaved if we took the title, summed up the last-day feeling, saying,

> Celebrations went on long after the final whistle – and why not? Newcastle are the new Allied Dunbar Premiership champions and Rob Andrew's men joined their Toon Platoon on the Harlequins pitch with the much-prized trophy.
>
> The Falcons fans flooded on to the pitch to carry off Andrew and the rest of the Newcastle team, and they went bananas as captain Dean Ryan held the trophy aloft. Chants of 'Are you watching, Saracens?' and 'Champions, champions' rang out as the Newcastle players sprayed champagne over each other, their fans and anyone within reach, and then they were chaired aloft again and threw their shirts to the supporters.
>
> Chairman Sir John Hall joined in and was immediately hoisted aloft with the trophy to the cheers of the crowd, who showed no signs of wanting to go home. It was a sight no one would have believed possible nearly three years ago when Sir John took over the ailing Newcastle Gosforth and brought in Andrew to transform the Tyneside club which has now been crowned Premiership champions.

Even without seeing much of the ball down the home straight, I felt there was still plenty to be proud of personally. Most notably I was chuffed at the fact that Newcastle came out on top having conceded fewer tries than any other team. That's where my pleasure lay, and there was enormous satisfaction to be gained from playing centre alongside either Inga Tuigamala or young Jonny Wilkinson. Also, the wingers listened to us, unlike my past experiences with Scotland where they wanted to do their own thing. At Newcastle everybody was happy to defend the way Inga and I wanted, which was straight up in the opposition's faces. Tony Underwood and Jim Naylor were especially good in that department. I believe we intimidated the opposition with our defence, and that was what gained us our success. Nor was it straight-up defence, either. We did a lot of scrambling defence with the forwards, Pat Lam and Richard Arnold especially, putting in some massive hits.

If there was a point where the league began to come into our sights, it was, I'm sure, a miserable mid-winter's day at Leicester around Christmas time. On a cold, wet night we came away with a morale-boosting 25–19 victory after taking all the Tigers could throw at us. It came as a shock to me afterwards, though, to realise that we had beaten Leicester as well as Bath away. I had honestly thought we would struggle as a team in the season after coming up from Division Two. And yet, an awareness of going into uncharted territory served to take the pressure off a bit, because our pre-season trip to France, where we immersed ourselves in quality fitness work and defeated the crack Agen club in a friendly, saw us set the realistic target of a top-four finish.

It was from the modest aim of proving wrong those who had written us off as a mid-table side that we developed. At the same time, though, I have to admit we carried a fair bit of luck, particularly at Gloucester, where we squeezed through 19–17 after seeing a Mark Mapletoft drop-goal attempt slide past the post in the closing moments. Other times when I thought it wasn't to be came at Saracens, where Michael Lynagh clinched the match for them with an injury-time drop goal, and at Wasps, where, uncharacteristically, Rob Andrew failed with a straightforward penalty.

All three of our defeats were suffered in London, and much discussion centred on that aspect of our record as the decision day at Harlequins neared. I had to acknowledge that travelling six hours by road was possibly the common factor in these defeats. Journeying by bus is tiring, which was another reason why I worried about so many of the team high-tailing it to Wembley. If Sir John Hall was trying to save a few quid on air fares, though, who could blame him? Sir John put so much into the club as it was and deserved to revel in any success. During the nail-biting run-in especially, he had gone through agonies up in the grandstand. Following the full-time whistle at Quins, he dashed down to the pitch and embraced the players.

Truth to tell, I almost felt embarrassed about the fact that when he stuck his head around the dressing-room door, Nick Popplewell and I greeted him with cries of 'Where's the bonus money?'. But it was meant in good spirit. Sir John was actually checking if the champagne had arrived and, realising the bubbly hadn't found its way down from the bar, disappeared and came back with bottle upon bottle of the stuff to be handed round. I was glad Steve Bates managed to inveigle an extra medal for Sir John, because the thing I like about him is that he mucks in. People think that wealth makes him untouchable. That's anything but the case.

The whole of English rugby owes a debt to Sir John. Of course, he is looking for a return on his investment, which is reckoned to have cost him £3.5 million in the 1997–98 season alone. Otherwise, why bother? But what he did was invest in personalities that the crowds wanted to see.

While respecting the author's right to express his views, I was turned off by a letter to the *Daily Telegraph* along the following lines shortly after our clinching win:

> The degree of media hype towards this mediocre outfit is quite beyond belief.
>
> They, like their footballing counterparts in the North-East, do not deserve any credit whatsoever for what they have achieved in their sport, or, to be more accurate, what Sir John Hall's millions have achieved.
>
> Pumping millions into a club, buying a world-class coach and team – there is no skill in that, and they deserve no respect.
>
> Credit and respect can be given to real clubs, clubs who have established themselves through hard work and effort: clubs like my own, Sale, and others like Wasps and Northampton.
>
> The ultimate irony could also have occurred. Had Wasps been relegated with Newcastle winning the league, the club who virtually robbed Wasps of a team would have perpetrated the greatest injustice. I thank God it didn't happen.
>
> But I suppose I should congratulate them: Newcastle on buying the Premiership trophy and Saracens for buying the Tetley Bitter Cup.

Each to his own view. As far as I am concerned, Sir John brought in 'names' such as Tuigamala, Armstrong and Weir and created a buzz and excitement through them to the extent that Kingston Park is no longer big enough at 8,000 capacity.

You need international matches, of course, to establish credibility and create the personalities the grass-roots fans relate to. You also need these internationals to define excellence from an independent perspective, and that is why there must be a balance between the club and country scene.

I disagreed with Scotland's director of rugby, Jim Telfer, when he accused the English club owners of trying to destroy the fabric of the game. They have injected a vibrancy never previously seen, and for the first time ever fans are behaving passionately about rugby union teams – the way I knew they did in rugby league.

It is well recorded that the 1997–98 rugby season ended for Sir John Hall in a blaze of glory at Harlequins on 16 May. Let me tell you, though, how the season had begun for Sir John, who had seen his five-year deadline for success shattered by three years. The season began when he and his wife, Lady Mae, travelled in our team bus to witness a highly encouraging 20–13 victory at Bath which sent out a warning that the new boys were not to be taken lightly. Buoyed up by victory, the team were boisterously making known their feelings about the long road trip home when Sir John ordered the driver to pull up outside a supermarket, where he personally supervised the purchase of around £200 worth of food and drink to ease any discomfort.

Sir John was the 16th Falcon, a man who simply revelled in the players' banter and proved he could take a bit of heckling himself. When, entering the New Year, Newcastle were drawn at Worcester in the cup on the same day that his Newcastle United football team were paired with Stevenage, it was rugby that proved the irresistible attraction. It's my understanding that Sir John simply felt more at ease amongst approachable rugby types – a situation which, I believe, reflects well on our game and the people in it.

Why not let the businessmen in elsewhere to drive the professional game? Provided they are honest, their presence can do nothing but good. They'll supply the drive and dynamism that will be needed in the new era. As well as the cash. I would be extremely worried for rugby union's future had Sir John and his fellow owners not emerged with several pluses from a battle with the Rugby Football Union which effectively ensured a club-based game, because the alternative was a structure vulnerable to stagnation. At least now, in England anyway, there will be a friction gap between clubs and governing body that can be the vehicle for taking the game forward. For, out of any disagreement, will probably come compromise, followed by advancement. Elsewhere they are proposing that the game should be run lock, stock and barrel by the Unions, which could effectively mean no real argument or debate ever taking place to throw up ideas. The club scene in England is surpassing all expectations, with gates up around 22 per cent in Division One last season. The owners should be congratulated, not shot down.

I base my views partly on the fact that I once came into a bit of money, necessitating a visit from a financial adviser. I must have listened to him for over half an hour, and it was clear the spiel was going right over my head. Breaking off the consultation, he told me, 'I'll look after your money and you play rugby. I wouldn't come to you and tell you how to play rugby.' We struck a bargain based on mutual respect, and that's the way it has to be.

I'm all for players being allowed to do just that and for coaches to concentrate on what they do best. As for the owners, they are the people with business acumen, and having put up their cash they will have a determination to succeed that the existing governing bodies will always struggle to match. Really, the governing bodies should be concentrating on administering the game and spending less time fretting about whether a club is liable to overcommit itself. That's the only way.

At one stage it appeared that Newcastle would enjoy the luxury of a canter to the finishing line. Those successive defeats at Saracens and Wasps put us on tenterhooks, before we revived the challenge with home wins over Bristol and Leicester followed by a nail-biting 20–15 success against Bath on a wretched night at Gateshead Stadium, where the narrower pitch does nothing for open, expansive rugby. Not that we were into that sort of approach, for reasons I've explained.

The Saracens and Wasps setbacks revived feelings that I've always been aware of – how much harder it is to play away than at home.

Don't ask me to put a finger on why; I've spent hours analysing the situation. But it's definitely there. Why else would coaches pore over videos of games and point out patterns that emerge involving playing either at home or away?

I've noticed that the way I run over an opponent's home pitch can be markedly different from how I perform in familiar surroundings. After a defeat at Richmond last season I spent an entire bus journey from London to Newcastle trying to work out exactly why I needed a familiar environment to perform to maximum capacity. I was up for that Richmond game, but I knew I wasn't performing, not putting tackles in or running into gaps the way I should have been. It must come from deep inside. I suppose it really is a question for the psychologists, because a pitch is, after all, a pitch. And they're all laid out on grass with posts at either end.

Richmond was one of the grounds on which we slipped up again in season 1997–98 and, as far as I'm concerned, it was the only place where we really let ourselves down. In every other match we were competing continuously, which helps explain why a bit of luck came our way. You have to be in with a shout to snatch a victory at the death, deserved or otherwise. Richmond was the single ground on which we were out of contention early.

Another of the most significant wins of the campaign for me, though, came at home to Saracens just three days after Scotland had gone down to England, and not just because they were to prove our closest challengers. Knowing I couldn't touch alcohol so close to a club match, I went straight home from the Murrayfield after-match reception. But I just couldn't bring myself to train with Newcastle on the Monday as arranged. I phoned Steve Black, the club fitness trainer, and explained my belief that part of being a professional athlete involves listening to your body – and mine was telling me to rest up. There was another reason, though, for opting out, and that was that I just couldn't face club-mates who had beaten me in an international hours earlier. I trusted them not to gloat. Nonetheless, I needed time to get over the England game mentally as well as physically.

As a player gets older he learns to understand his body and how far to push it. I went down to Kingston Park on the Tuesday and had half an hour's run but nothing at all strenuous. By the Wednesday I was as fresh as a daisy and had one of my best games of the season. Doddie Weir and Gary Armstrong, who had been thinking along the same lines as me, felt the same way. Speaking after the game to Steve Black and also our physio, Martin Brewer, they were complimentary – and not, I hope, because we won. Players are their main interest and Blacky sent us all a letter at the end of that week, offering congratulations. He told me in his note, 'Alan, the one thing I have learned about you is that you know your own body.'

The season had its controversies, that's for sure, and I wasn't at all enamoured with Northampton putting out a desperately weakened team against our only challengers Saracens at the tail-end of the season. I lost respect for them that day. I expected better from the Saints who, with nothing to play for, just seemed to lie down, in contrast to when we had played them at Franklins Gardens in a Tetley Bitter Cup quarter-final and they seemed to go overboard about victory. Ian McGeechan, the Northampton coach, had done his homework on us before that match and delegated Tim Rodber to stand out among the backs at lineouts to mark Inga Tuigamala on the charge. That curtailed our cutting edge and no mistake, because quick ruck ball was at a premium. But at full-time you'd have thought Northampton had won the cup, and several players embarrassed themselves by shedding tears of delight. Others were running around the pitch like dervishes. For goodness sake! All Northampton had done, in fact, was produce a one-off performance, and they promptly bowed out of the cup to Saracens in the next round. I wasn't surprised. Teams that celebrate too loudly before the job is done need to take a good, hard look at themselves.

Another match memorable for the wrong reasons came when we went to Perpignan in the European Conference and found ourselves pelted by bottles and spit from the home fences. Fortunately we produced one of our best displays *en route* to reaching the semi-finals to shut them up, and it was a measure of our competence that they went on to reach the French Cup final, losing to Stade Français.

The biggest individual controversies affecting Newcastle concerned the alleged biting of Leicester flanker Neil Back by our prop Paul van Zandvliet, and skipper Dean Ryan becoming the first player to be sin-binned under a new ruling. Eddie Butler, writing in *The Observer*, said it appeared Paul had been trying to devour Back whole, which summed up the ludicrous nature of the charge, because if he'd wanted to take a chunk out of him he'd surely have chosen a soft, fleshy part. 'Tanky' van Zandvliet, as we call him, is a tough hombre who has had to work for everything that has come his way, including a spell as a fisherman. I could envisage 'Tanky' standing on an opponent who was lying on the ball but cannibalism isn't in his nature, and I was relieved and delighted when a disciplinary inquiry decided there was insufficient video evidence to support the allegations made against him.

If the bookies had been quoting odds on the first player to be sin-binned, I have to say Dean Ryan would have started odds-on favourite. Dean duly obliged against London Irish, but later in the season his outstanding commitment was recognised with a return to the England team for the Calcutta Cup match with Scotland at Murray-field. It was such a shame, too, that concussion sustained five days earlier meant Dean had to be ruled out of our last match and therefore couldn't be on the pitch at full-time.

A sin bin does calm players down, in my experience, and offers a reminder to the over-aggressive individual that he needs to take a grip on himself. Also, if you get somebody who is a persistent infringer in terms of killing the ball, it is a good thing to get him off for ten minutes to help sort the game out. Once binned, the culprit can reflect on his offence and come back and play rugby – which is what people pay to see. If teams slow the ball down illegally against opponents with good backs, it doesn't benefit the spectacle. What I particularly like about the concept is that players serve a punishment against the team they committed the offence against.

When I returned from rugby league I was convinced that I'd have a significant edge on my new training partners at Newcastle, including Dean Ryan. I can't overstate the shock I got when I went into the gym and saw how hard the forwards trained. All right, Ryan, with his military background, might have been used to physical toil, and the same went for other ex-soldiers in Garath Archer and George Graham. But the work done by the likes of Doddie Weir, Ross Nesdale, Richard Arnold and others was a real eye-opener. The strength and endurance shown particularly by Ryan was phenomenal. I wouldn't have liked to have worked under him in the Army and been taken out for runs every morning, that's for sure.

On my return from rugby league, one of the things I had to work on was going to ground and presenting the ball in the tackle. In the rival code we could simply hit the deck and know we would be allowed up on our feet to play the ball. Ryan was a marvellously patient tutor as I sought to rediscover old ways. A big, physical, aggressive type who rarely takes a backward step, Dean, a bit of an icon on Tyneside recently, put me in mind of Kurt Sorensen at Widnes. Sorensen was another man who knew how to get over the advantage line through being robust when taking the ball into the tackle.

Having said all that, Newcastle would have wrapped up the title earlier had our discipline been tighter, and Dean was a leading culprit at times. Rugby union is still a long way behind rugby league in the realm of self-discipline, and Newcastle players consistently gave away penalties when in possession. In league that is punishable with a fine. Similarly, talking back to the referee, always a futile exercise, hits rugby league players hard in the pocket.

If the most consistent Newcastle forward over the season in my book was the Western Samoan Pat Lam, deservedly voted Premiership player of the season, then much credit should also go to Doddie Weir for coming through an indifferent spell to finish with a flourish just when it was needed. Doddie's early form was undoubtedly governed by the knee injury suffered on the British Lions tour when he was brutally kicked by the Mpumalanga forward Marius Bosman. That type of unprovoked blow can easily affect a player's confidence. Hopefully, Doddie has now fully matured, although it wasn't so long ago that Scotland coach Jim Telfer noted how easily the second row could slip into 'big, daft laddie' mode. Telfer made a point of telling Doddie before the England match this year that it was the hard-nosed professional he wanted to see in action. I could certainly see where Jim was coming from, because I had made a similar point a year earlier to Doddie when he was voted Famous Grouse Scottish Player of the Five Nations Championship. In congratulating Doddie I urged him to think not just about having great seasons but, primarily, a great career.

I certainly had contrasting types as centre partners over the season, with Jonny Wilkinson becoming, at 18, the youngest player to be capped for England in 70 years when he went on as a substitute late in a match against Ireland. A precocious talent if ever there was one,

Wilkinson helped offset criticism that the Newcastle side were in danger of growing old together.

My more regular partner, however, was Inga Tuigamala, and I especially liked the way he acknowledged that rugby league had made him the player he is today even though he had already won All Black honours before changing codes. Inga is quick to admit that when he initially switched he found the players far tougher than he had imagined they would be. Indeed, it took him a lengthy spell of adjustment at Wigan merely to get his fitness up to scratch. A practising Christian, Inga does, however, preach a lot, and when we first met up at Newcastle he used to shake his head in disgust at me because of my swearing, which I know he doesn't like. I'm trying to curb the colourful language, Inga. Honest. Don't give up on me.

Seriously, Inga is one of the few players I've come across to whom it makes no difference whether he plays at home or away, and I'd love to take him around the country, showing him off as a role model to youngsters. My curiosity, incidentally, about the home and away factor has extended to studying team-mates and watching the little things they do on team buses and in the dressing-room. Everything Inga does week in, week out by way of preparation is identical, and the same goes for Gary Armstrong.

Gary is a 110 per cent trier who can never be knocked down for long. He has been dropped and he has come back. He has had bad injuries and overcome them. I had Gary Armstrong as a training partner from the moment I returned from league and Rob could not have given me anybody harder to measure myself against. Gary is exactly the same as me – competitive in everything he does – and our skirmishes were a throwback to my days at Leeds when I would throw down the gauntlet to Ellery Hanley. Gary is the perfect club player and never shirks any challenge. I like to think we share the same approach to many things. At Newcastle he is, quite simply, the driving force who was deserving of the captaincy for our final match in the regrettable absence of Ryan.

The one occasion on which Gary let his standards drop was when he had to turn out against Worcester in the Tetley Bitter Cup 24 hours after playing in Scotland's 25–21 defeat by Italy in Treviso. I was excused duty but lack of cover at scrum-half saw Gary put in a difficult situation, which he faced with typical tenacity.

Gary was made Scotland captain after the Italy match, when my name was again mentioned as a contender. Earlier in the season there was talk of either me or Andy Nicol getting the job, but I let it be known in advance that the selectors would be better to go with a younger player, and it was the same when it came to falling in behind Gary, as far as I was concerned. It was, though, funny travelling together to Newcastle and winding each other up at a time when both of us were being tipped for the Scottish team captaincy. I'd tell Gary I was convinced he had the job and he would say he'd heard it the other way. When the decision was announced I was on the phone straightaway and said, 'You knew all the time, you bugger . . .' He denied having had his card marked, but I'm not so sure. Gary can keep things to himself when he wants to.

Well before we went to Wembley for the match with Wales in 1998 and before I knew Gary would be captain, I was telling him it is one of the best places you can play rugby. I've always wanted to walk up those Wembley steps and collect a cup. Failing that, I'd love to lead a team out at Wembley, I said. Ellery Hanley had let Gary Schofield take Leeds out in recognition of the fact he'd been at the club ten years, and I wonder if that is where my thought came from. Anyway, I mentioned that to Gary and speculated with him whether Rob Wainwright (then captain) would let me lead the team out. Circumstances dictated that by the time we got to Wembley Gary had succeeded Rob as captain, and I spent a long time as the game approached wondering if my remarks had been taken on board. If they had been filed away, though, Gary said nothing, and he led the team out himself – although not for a moment did I begrudge him that opportunity. Why, four matches into his captaincy Gary is still awaiting the chance to lead Scotland out at Murrayfield, since his two home appearances have coincided with 50th caps for Tony Stanger and Doddie Weir.

Anyway, I made sure I was second in the line – right behind Gary – when we walked out at Wembley. I decided I would get as close to the front of the line as I could to savour the roar of the crowd. Gary would have gone down a bundle in rugby league and I know Doug Laughton had a nibble, but Gary didn't respond to his tentative signing offer. An offer from Newcastle director of rugby Rob Andrew was different, because Gary was in a position to remain in his beloved home town of Jedburgh and travel across the border. The same applied to me and my new bungalow at Stitchill, outside Kelso, built by my Dad pending the return of Clan Tait from rugby league.

I wouldn't have blamed Rob Andrew if, having noted an initial interest in me, he had run the proverbial mile on hearing about the contractual mess I was in at Leeds rugby league club. Basically the complication stemmed from my contract with Super League, which guaranteed me a loyalty payment on 2 July 1996 – my birthday. The deal had been agreed in two parts, with £100,000 due in year one, followed by the further instalment. In fact, I never got any pleasure from gaining that money, because the first cheque arrived while my son was in hospital recovering from his cancer operation and it lay untouched behind a vase on the mantelpiece for weeks. The second payment of £50,000 was the subject of a bitter wrangle.

I'd fallen out of favour at Leeds, who were prepared to let me go if I, in turn, was prepared to waive my contract with them. Not a problem, as far as I was concerned. However, I still had the Super League money due from the governing body, which I felt well entitled to because at the time it was offered I had expressed my loyalty and my name had been used extensively to help sell the revolutionary concept of summer rugby and so on. Leeds were happy to let me train with Newcastle, but the rugby league authorities just couldn't accept releasing me from that contract before the full period of the deal with them had elapsed. The end result was a stalemate, because there was no way I could get back even close to the form I was capable of under Leeds coach Dean Bell.

On Rob Andrew's instructions the Newcastle fitness trainer, Steve Black, really put me through the mill to see if I still had it in me to make the grade back in rugby union. Blacky said straightaway that I was phenomenally fit, even though I considered myself only halfway there due to the toe operation I'd undergone the previous season. I was so keen to sign that I concealed the agony I felt running up and down the steps of the Newcastle United football ground at St James' Park.

All would have been well had Maurice Lindsay, the Chief Executive of Super League, not stepped in to declare I was going nowhere until I paid back some of the money I had been given. Even then a deal could have been brokered between Newcastle and the

Super League authorities until they set the figure at £50,000, an amount which nearly floored Rob who, naturally, began to wonder if I was worth all the hassle. I'd have been happy to have played on at Leeds had the coach not been intent on getting me out, and after Lindsay's intervention it was just a matter of digging in.

All the time this was going on, though, I was getting paid by Leeds who were, understandably, fuming at the outlay. In the end Maurice Lindsay gave in under pressure from the old Leeds board after I'd taken every opportunity to state to them I wanted to go home to Scotland and, effectively, retirement. What really brought things to a head was when I went back home to represent the Scotland rugby league team in that match against Ireland in Glasgow. Interviewed afterwards, I was asked if, because rugby union had just gone professional, I would like to return to that code. I went on record saying that I would because I was not getting on well with Leeds, and John Beattie reported me in *The Herald* as saying, 'I am unhappy at Leeds and I can't play rugby when I am unhappy. My wife and family are already back in Scotland and I would want to come back to a club. But I wouldn't need the same kind of money that I have been on at Leeds. I would want to join a club that was ambitious and had plans. The next two or three weeks are vital for me, as I want to find out if I can leave Leeds or not.'

Returning to Headingley, I was confronted by Hugh McGahan, who handed me an envelope containing a letter which said, 'We have stopped your contract because we feel you are not giving the club 100 per cent.' I was livid and threatened legal action. An early port of call was my agent, who had been told that because of the way I had played against Ireland the Leeds management had reason to believe I had not been giving them my all. I responded by saying I couldn't produce the goods for Bell and McGahan because they were incapable of showing me respect and were not treating me as though they wanted me. The compromise was a fine, after the club acknowledged they couldn't stop my wages, and I braced myself to pay a modest £50. That was all I expected – after all, I had played for Scotland for nothing and it had actually cost me money to travel to Glasgow. In fact, the club fined me £500.

Out of sheer frustration I phoned the rugby league authorities, appealing for support because they had asked me to play and push the sport in unfamiliar surroundings. But they backed Leeds, who insisted I ought to have been turning out for their reserves rather than indulging in missionary work on behalf of rugby league. So, with my agent insisting I should cut my losses and pay, it actually cost me £500 to represent Scotland. I'll never forgive the Leeds management for doing that to me, nor will I forgive the rugby league authorities, who knew I was flag-waving for them. But at least I had taken out a £500 advertisement back home, drawing attention to my difficulties at Leeds in a come-and-get-me plea to rugby union.

One of the first to grasp the nettle and enter the bidding were Heriot's FP, a famous Edinburgh old boys' side who went 'open' in the '70s. I'd heard too that Boroughmuir, another leading Edinburgh rugby union club, perhaps better placed to succeed in future because they are not tied to a school, were sniffing around. Once Newcastle became serious bidders for my services, however, it was no contest, because, with all due respect to the Edinburgh club scene, I knew that at Newcastle I'd be in top-class company. Nevertheless, Alan Campbell accurately reported in the *Daily Express* just prior to my competitive début in a 51–10 fifth-round Pilkington Cup win over West Hartlepool, 'Instead of wearing the colours of Sir John Hall at Newcastle this weekend, former Scotland and Great Britain rugby union and rugby league international Alan Tait could have been playing on a Scottish Premiership ground.'

Campbell went on to link me with Boroughmuir before quoting me as saying that the absence of relegation in the Scottish League for one year only would reduce competition and therefore my chances of a hasty return to the international scene.

George Graham, an old rugby league adversary who could have done a lot better for himself than sign for Carlisle if he had not been piqued at missing out on the 1991 Scotland World Cup squad, had already signed for Newcastle. I've no doubt George vouched for me with Rob Andrew, whom I was determined to reward if he were to sign me, and, as I later discovered, it was no bad thing having a friend at court.

One of the reasons Steve Black had put me through the hoop and required me to run up and down the terracing at St James' Park football ground was because John Bentley had been dropping broad hints that I was finished on account of the foot injury which had seen me go under Louis Stoddart's knife. Bentley, apparently, had a mate, Simon Irvine, who had been at Leeds with me and whom he had wanted to play alongside at Newcastle. I wondered why Steve Black had tested me out so much. I learned why after John Bentley had left to join Rotherham . . .

Bad weather meant that several weeks elapsed before I could slip back into rugby union, after Leeds finally let me go following 126 appearances which yielded 44 tries. The official announcement came in the following terms from then club spokesman Stuart Duffy, now of Bradford Bulls, who said, 'Alan leaves the club with our best wishes. He is coming to the end of his career and he felt a move nearer to his family would be in his best interests. Alan has been a great servant to Leeds and we would like to wish him every success in the future.'

I had made some remarks for the sake of the press release about wanting to finish my career in junior rugby union development in Scotland. In fact it was Newcastle who were on the horizon, and things finally started happening when Rob took me to play with him for Mickey Steele-Bodger's XV in the annual match which formed part of Cambridge University's preparations for their Twickenham showdown with Oxford.

I was picked on the wing for a match we won 54–38 after travelling down the motorway in Rob's car on what actually proved to be the start of the road back to Murrayfield. I quickly got into the Newcastle side, and a début against West Hartlepool, a match watched by Richie Dixon, the Scotland coach, attracted much attention back home. One of the first off the mark was Alasdair Reid in the *Sunday Times*. Alasdair drew parallels between my return to international rugby union and a similar move undertaken by Jonathan Davies. I told him, 'Jonathan is just a little man but he'll do anything to get to the top. I'm exactly the same. I love the challenge and I always want to prove I'm better than others. I'm keen to get back in with Scotland. The quicker I get playing for Newcastle, the better for me.'

At the same time I was realistic enough to note in the wake of some criticism directed against Bath converts Henry Paul and Jason Robinson, 'There are people who want to find faults in the former league guys and who want us to fail. I've never said that I'm going to set the world on fire in rugby union and I told Rob Andrew that when he signed me, but I'm a solid player and a team player.'

My former Scotland colleague Alan Tomes, who lives on Tyneside, also sowed a few seeds which led to Newcastle taking an interest in my position. Above all, though, I owe a big debt of gratitude to Rob Andrew, who gave me my big chance back in rugby union amongst some great players, aided by two shrewd coaches in Steve Bates and Dean Ryan. Rob was a good friend right up until my final match for Newcastle, the Sanyo Challenge against a World XV at Twickenham at the end of the 1997–98 season.

We had mutually agreed the previous evening that it was time for me to move on, and Rob asked me to captain the side on my farewell appearance. It was a marvellous gesture, especially as that match remains my one and only appearance at Twickenham, and I was required to step up and receive the challenge trophy surrounded by well-wishers. What a difference from the way I departed from Leeds rugby league club, alone and unheralded. It was such a good feeling to know, through Rob's actions, that my contribution had been appreciated. As for that fine which paved the way for my leaving rugby league, well, perhaps it was a case of honours even.

Years ago, while at Widnes, I kept a greyhound called Mr Tatters, which I used to run at tracks around the North-West. One night Maurice Lindsay was standing at Bolton and happily shouting '4–1' at me, implying that Mr Tatters had no chance. Maurice thought there was no way my dog could give away four metres in a handicap, but I promptly marched up and gave him £100 to stick in his pocket until after the race. Mr Tatters came roaring home, and it was a real highlight to take the money off Maurice. Maybe he was just intent on getting his money back before releasing me for one of the most exciting – and totally unexpected – phases of my sporting career!

CHAPTER SEVEN

Foxes and Lions

I'm told it's common these days for a left winger to feel uncomfortable when brought into the bosom of people who run this Labour government. What I do know is that as left winger for the British Lions rugby team which claimed a Test series triumph against the world champion Springboks, I felt my principles would not allow me to attend a party in our honour at No. 10 Downing Street shortly after returning from the high veldt.

Normally I am one of the most apolitical of people. But between wrapping up the series and the end of 1997, something happened which was to raise my hackles and ensure that Prime Minister Tony Blair's invitation remained on the mantelpiece. There are many places I'd have followed the victorious 1997 British Lions to for the sake of a reunion, but a gathering hosted by New Labourites wasn't one of them.

I felt it would have been hypocritical to have strolled into No. 10 and nibbled a few canapés with MPs representing a party whose Minister of Sport, Tony Banks, had pledged to ensure fox hunting would be banned before the next general election. What's more, I was delighted when a parliamentary private members' bill which would have imposed major restraints on how we use the countryside fell through because of lack of debating time. The countryside has always been a big part of my life and I've seen the damage caused by foxes. To me the hunt is as civilised a way as any of controlling them, besides being a source of exercise for hounds, horses and riders.

I guess that's my knighthood gone down the Swanee, but so what? The private members' bill needed careful thought, otherwise any dog owner whose pet kills a rabbit could have been liable for prosecution, as I understand it. On the whole politics is something I'm ambivalent about. But when parties even consider legislation which could stop me going for walks in the countryside with my dogs for fear that they could catch a rabbit and I'd end up being prosecuted, that's when I sit up.

Call me petty. Call me a party pooper. But that's just the way I felt, and 250,000 people turned up at a rally in London to express similar feelings. I've seen people go out at night and shoot foxes. That, to me, is slaughter. With hunting the strong fox has a chance of escaping, which means it is usually the weak who get snared anyway. Hunting isn't as cruel as it seems, and there were also a sizeable number of jobs set to be lost if the Countryside Bill had been approved.

Having got that off my chest . . . If my Lions tour ended on a controversial note, it more or less began in rather unusual circumstances too:

'My name's Jerry Guscott. You don't fart or snore, do you?'

Yes, the star of both the 1989 and 1993 British Lions tours had his own unique way of welcoming a newcomer on safari, especially one who was to be his room-mate for a week prior to flying out to South Africa in May 1997.

It was to prove a historic tour for the Lions, and a journey of discovery for me from the moment that introduction to Jerry left me wondering what it was about English centre three-quarters that made them so fascinated with breaking wind, bearing in mind Will Carling's memorable branding of the entire England committee as '57 old farts'.

I'd heard a bit about Guscott before we first met, notably from Rob Andrew, my boss at Newcastle Falcons, who had said, 'Jerry's all right when he wants to be. At other times he has a chip on his shoulder.' There were occasions on tour when I found Guscott, for all that he could be good company, actually had a fish supper on his shoulder, never mind a mere chip! That gut feeling was to intensify when I returned home and read that he felt I hadn't been pulling my weight on the training paddock.

But our initial encounter was convivial enough, and his reaction as I turned the key and entered the room at least broke the ice for the week of team-building that was to follow. Looking back, though, I really can't believe I made such a conscious effort to get onside with

Mr High and Mighty Guscott. Maybe if he'd slogged it out at Featherstone on a wet Tuesday in December he might have been entitled to that sort of respect from me. All he really seemed to care about, and in a thoroughly self-centred way, was whether I farted in my sleep, for goodness sake. I might have played rugby league for money, Jerry old chap, but I knew the social graces.

As I stretched out on my bed that first night with the Lions, taking extra care not to break wind and disturb my colleague, I struggled to comprehend the latest amazing twist my career was taking after returning from rugby league. Honestly, it was *Roy of the Rovers*, Alf Tupper and Wilson of *The Wizard* all rolled into one. What must they have been thinking at Leeds, my former rugby league club, who were convinced I was heading off back to Scotland and a future coaching rugby union to youngsters? Of course, a few months earlier my Lions selection had been predicted – but only by my Dad. Who else? My greatest fan and critic had insisted, 'You're not going back to rugby union just for fun. You'll be on that British Lions tour to South Africa. Mark my words.'

When Lions manager Fran Cotton set a precedent and announced a provisional squad of 62 players which included me midway through the Five Nations Championship, it was a major shock as far as I was concerned. Never mind the masses. I hadn't got any further than an appearance for Scotland A when Fran included me in his plans, although I did have a slight inkling I could be summering on the high veldt. Out of the blue a letter had arrived asking me if I was available for the Lions and, if so, what positions I played. Ever eager to oblige, I filled in my positions as full-back, centre or wing, emphasising versatility and somehow forgetting to volunteer as a prop forward. I then rushed the form straight back.

After that all I had to do was get into the Scotland team, show a bit of form and stay injury-free – which was easier said than done, and it was on the last count that I was so nearly found wanting. Fortunately a knee ligament strain did not prove as serious as first feared, and so there I was, at the court of King Jerry, trying hard not to make a rude noise after another scare on the day the squad was announced.

I was sure my chance had gone when the postie passed my house and offered a few words of commiseration. He must have known it was a big day for me. In fact, the holiday brochures were even scattered around our house when Caroline and I sat down to watch the announcement of the squad live on television. We thought it was just a matter of hearing formal confirmation that I had been overlooked and then settling on a destination to take the kids – so I was stunned to hear my name read out. Postal communications between the Lions' den and the Scottish Borders had not been the best, but the televised announcement, although more public, sparked equally joyous celebrations.

Actually, one of the real bonuses of our preliminary week's gathering at Weybridge was the chance for me to get to know the other former rugby league pros in the party – Scott Quinnell, Allan Bateman, Scott Gibbs, John Bentley and David Young. This might seem strange to a lot of folk, but I had learned very quickly in league that opposition players are the enemy and fraternisation is greeted with suspicion, if not actively discouraged. In union, however, old habits die hard, and when the England team opted to fly home soon after this year's Calcutta Cup match at Murrayfield rather than stick around for a night on the town, the situation provoked raised eyebrows and the odd editorial comment.

While I had rarely shared a pint with the other ex-league boys, I had shared a pitch with them, and I knew who in the Lions party merited most respect. Allan Bateman, for example, had gone out to Australia and proved himself with the Cronulla club. No mean feat. Scott Gibbs was another out of the top drawer and one player I felt I would get on well with, for when I was being touted for a return to the Scotland set-up he had said some kind things in the press about my abilities. Hopefully I managed to reciprocate Scott's words of encouragement when fate dealt him a cruel blow during the tour. John Bentley was another old adversary from league whose abilities I was even more familiar with, through sharing a dressing-room at Newcastle Falcons.

So, the rugby league influence that was to be subsequently praised by forwards coach Jim Telfer – a man who, I had long suspected, had a bit of a downer on the 13-a-side code but whose broad-mindedness and sheer professionalism I grew to respect in spades – was there from the outset. Maybe that wasn't too surprising, either, since coach Ian McGeechan had grown up in Leeds surrounded by rugby league, while manager Fran Cotton had a similar background across the Pennines in Lancashire.

Before the tour I got an inkling that McGeechan had been picking the brains of Shaun McRae, coach at St Helens. It proved time well spent. A lot of defensive drills were brought in. I know too that the Lions got a buzz from practising these drills wearing body armour which might have made them look like Ninja Turtles but which allowed the action situations to be better simulated. Such accessories were new in union but had been used in league for years, and proof of their worth came with every stitch and bandage which had to be applied. It showed the lads were getting stuck in during the run-outs.

Fran is renowned for blunt talking, but I also found him to be a sharp listener. Fortunately he lent me his ear before the tour was up and running. The ex-league contingent had their views sought on various matters, and I stressed the value of communication as well as the need to stay a foot behind the ten metres offside line. Many an opposition overlap was nipped in the bud, too, by an ability to wrap up man and ball in the tackle. That was a speciality of Gibbs, and I dare say it was pointed out that in seeking to dislodge the ball one of the hardest parts of the body to use as a lever is the front of the wrist.

Another thing league had taught me was that players had to be respected as individuals so long as they produced the goods on the pitch, which is where it mattered. For example, Ellery Hanley refused to attend functions, and people would knock him for that. But the fact that Ellery was his own man helped to make him perhaps the greatest player of his generation. You could never tell Ellery – or Martin Offiah, for that matter – what to do. Yet in a game they would do everything and anything for a team-mate.

While having no difficulty recognising the skills of a rugby league player, Fran Cotton, I reckoned, was bound hand and foot by the traditions of rugby union when we first met, and that certainly didn't augur well for a successful mission. To his lasting credit, Fran learned to be flexible and gave us our heads. But if he hadn't adapted, I fear the Lions would have been placed in a strait-jacket of rules and regulations to the extent that they wouldn't have been able to function effectively.

Initially I found it amusing that Fran would frequently refer back to his own playing career, in which – give credit where it's due – he made his mark as a prop forward in a winning Lions Test side against the Springboks in 1974. But that was Fran's benchmark, and what worked then wasn't guaranteed to work more than two decades on. If those '74 Lions had frequent team meetings, then so too must the class of '97. At least, that seemed to be the philosophy.

At these gatherings guidelines emerged and quickly multiplied. Before we knew it there was a list of dos and don'ts the length of a goal-post at King's Park, Durban – which, as any rugby 'anorak' will confirm, are among the highest in the world. Most of what was apparently set in stone prior to our tour seemed petty, the stuff real pros shouldn't bother about.

I'd been lucky to spend most of my time in league under Doug Laughton, a coach who occasionally took me into his confidence. Not only did Doug teach me about tactics, he also had a way with people and had learned how to get them on his side. Using Doug's tried and tested teachings, I responded in a way Fran might not have expected when he asked if I thought his team meetings were worth while. I said yes, which was what he wanted to hear. But I then undermined his philosophy to an extent by adding that the rules these meetings produced were in danger of going too far. I offered as an example the notion that players must be constantly mixing. This wasn't something we had bothered about on the Great Britain rugby league tour I'd been on seven years earlier. I told Fran that while a fear of cliques developing was admirable, stopping guys socialising with their mates was liable to be damaging. I just couldn't imagine a league tour on which the Wigan lads, for example, were informed they couldn't be seen together in groups. 'If I make a friend on this trip and you say we can't knock around together because we constitute a clique, I'll be upset,' I told Fran.

In my experience, tour management shouldn't lean too heavily on pros. All that should matter is that the players are at the right mental pitch for training and matches. And it was on the pitch that the Lions had to bond. I even went so far as to claim that outwith training and playing, team members should really be allowed to do as they wanted. Far better to encourage individual thinking that way than to risk churning out clones unable to make decisions or even think for themselves. I've seen it happening in so many sports, particularly on trips, where the players are herded to the extent that they are told precisely what to eat and what to wear at all times. From the moment players get up in the morning until their heads hit the pillow at night, their lives are ruled by officials who would happily breathe for them if given the chance. Thankfully the Lions management pulled back from the brink of being like that, and players had scope to be themselves.

Very occasionally, however, a 'treat them like schoolboys' mentality did prevail, although it was well down the chain of command from Fran Cotton. I know that the Lions set out as a team and achieved what they did as a team, and it ill behoves anyone to break ranks and criticise now. But I really didn't appreciate being told to alter training schedules that served me well, and for the sake of those who follow on future tours I feel obliged to mention this aspect of the trip.

In begging to differ from the prescribed system now and again, I was relieved to get full backing from Ian McGeechan. I had my own routine and Geech appreciated that. For example, being taught different tricks with weights over the relatively short period of time covered by the tour was not going to help me give it my absolute best shot when it came to beating the Springboks – which was, after all, the objective.

Fitness sheets were drawn up and circulated, and some of the ideas were quite good. But, at the end of the day, everybody was free to incorporate what they fancied into their personal regimes. Once again, I stress that a professional regime is largely down to self-discipline. Not that Jerry Guscott saw things quite the same way. While I had explained to Geech that, at the age of 32 going on 33, I could see myself succeeding only in 'blowing up' on the training field if I went full pelt virtually every day, Jerry appeared to know best. Geech was happy to admit that what I said about avoiding two- or three-hour run-outs every day made sense, as long as I produced the goods on the field. He even went further and acknowledged that there would be other players similarly placed. While Geech was guided by Dr James Robson, our medical officer, Jerry Guscott appeared to be motivated by something else – a fear of being upstaged, perhaps? In his book chronicling the tour, Jerry went so far as to accuse me of being the 'master of the six-day injury'. An injury which, remarkably, cleared up just in time for me to play a match without having put in the spadework beforehand.

Now I quite understand why some of my fellow Lions, particularly the younger ones, thought I had been given the equivalent of a gold card. Maybe it even seemed a bit unfair that I was doing three sessions a week in the gym to their three hours a day of solid graft. But I still did the business when it mattered, I would contend, thanks partly to drawing on lessons learned at the hands of those sporting maestros, the Australian Kangaroos rugby league team. My insight dated back to 1992 when the Kangaroos came over and were granted training facilities at the gym used by my club, Leeds. While outsiders were barred during these sessions, the Leeds players had access, and I could see for myself how hard the Kangaroos trained. I learned most of all that they trained harder in the gym than outside on the pitch, and also that by early in the tour they were merely topping up their fitness levels.

Bolstering fitness was something I could do satisfactorily on my own, and I couldn't have been shirking when I acquired the catchphrase 'Taity's off to the gym'. Could I? The phrase became a trademark, and it was with these very words that Paul Wallace greeted me at full-time when Ireland played Scotland last season. I was flattered.

What I feared about over-training was the fact that I was out of contract with Newcastle and one injury could leave me washed up without any income. In the short term, anyway. As a professional, this preyed on my mind, and if the Scottish Rugby Union had really been switched on at that stage, my fears wouldn't have arisen. When I flew out with the Lions to South Africa I was on the brink of signing with the SRU to join one of their four district teams, probably the Border Reivers. In fact, the SRU and I talked and talked. And then we talked some more. The trouble was – and here's something the SRU could maybe learn from rugby league – they didn't know how to strike when the iron was hot and clinch a deal.

In my experience, when professional people – whether they are Doug Laughton of Widnes or the Australian Rugby League representative charged with signing players to spoil Super League – talk turkey, they are always properly prepared with contracts at the ready if necessary. Once you have an agreement it is pure folly to leave a player for a period in which he can only change his mind. The Scottish Rugby Union could have had my signature on the basis of terms discussed at length, but their negotiator then had to go and consult with somebody else, and I'd wager that a major committee would end up having a say on whether or not to negotiate my terms. That's no way to do business in the world of modern professional sport, but I accept that I was maybe not what the SRU were looking for anyway, given their budget restraints. My eagerness to pass on experience particularly in the realm of fitness training and conditioning remains undiminished, however. Maybe one day . . .

Anyway, with the SRU still pondering about whether or not to make me an offer, I set out for South Africa, where I was relieved to find that other signing options were available. Indeed, they began to multiply. Ian McGeechan made it clear he would find a place for me at his club, Northampton. And another of the Lions coaching panel, Andy Keast, offered me a deal with Harlequins and even stated that I could move into fitness training with them when my playing days ended. I was absolutely astounded by such attractive options, but it was important I first talked with Rob Andrew about renewing my Newcastle contract, because he was the person who gave me my big chance back in rugby union in the first place. I owe Rob a lot for that, and I also owe Ian McGeechan for the faith he showed by bringing me on the Lions tour.

I was determined to repay both men before we stepped off the plane back in London. The attitude I took to South Africa was that I didn't care what happened (within reason, of course) as long as I did the business on the pitch. I had, however, known frustration and failure on a tour with the Great Britain rugby league team to New Zealand and Papua New Guinea in 1990, and the desire not to suffer a repeat experience was a massive motivation. On that rugby league tour I played two Tests against the Papua New Guineans but was flown home injured before the big stuff against the Kiwis. I fell out with Maurice Lindsay, the tour manager, as well as members of the coaching staff because I couldn't put the work in on the training field before they realised I was suffering from a condition known as Gilmore's Groin. That meant my stomach wall was torn, so no wonder I was having problems – although, to be fair, it was a difficult condition to diagnose. More has been learned now due to high-profile casualties such as footballer Alan Shearer.

So, I went out with the Lions determined to prove to myself that

I could come through a tour. And come through it well. But when I stopped and looked around, I suddenly realised that the strength of competition for team places was awesome. Will Greenwood was an uncapped centre but I had played against him in a Newcastle v. Leicester match and knew he was really coming through in a hurry. Jerry Guscott was an automatic choice, while both Gibbs and Bateman were bound to be there or thereabouts come the three-Test series, if fit.

My first chance came in the match against Border at East London, when I got on as a 45th-minute substitute and played well in an 18–14 win. Then, before the next outing, came near calamity. I almost blew my big opportunity to make an early impression through sending my kit on to the next destination while I set off for a couple of post-match drinks. Sending kit on ahead was standard practice because the aircraft used for internal flights are so small. But while word went out after the game to John Bentley and a couple of others that they were involved next up and should have a quiet night with the emphasis on rest, no such directions were given to me. The next morning, as I shuffled to breakfast in my flip-flops, I encountered Ian McGeechan, who wondered why I wasn't in my kit – which was, of course, by now hundreds of miles away. I ended up borrowing boots from Matt Dawson and got through the training session before flying on to Cape Town and a showdown with Western Province.

This was a huge game against a team containing Percy Montgomery, a real star on the Springboks' subsequent tour of Europe. I came off the field cock-a-hoop following our 38–21 win and relishing the fact I'd been pushed to the limits for the first time since leaving rugby league. I got a try and knew I had played well before being subbed by Will Greenwood eight minutes before the end.

Andy Keast, who was, of course, chasing me to join Harlequins, provided the confirmation of how I felt. He said, 'Keep playing like that and you're pushing for a Test place.' I was sceptical, but Andy told me he had been speaking with James Small, now South Africa's top try-scorer in Tests and a star winger with Western Province. Keast knew Small from time spent in Durban working with the Natal team, and although their conversation had centred on an alleged eye-gouging incident involving John Bentley, the subject eventually changed to the composition of the Lions squad. Small maintained that the player he most respected was the, ahem, baby-faced kid in the centre. Baby-faced? I was 32 years old, for goodness sake!

Keast persisted with his flattery by claiming Small had rated me man of the match. I thought that wasn't a bad accolade for someone like me who was playing only about his 20th match back in rugby union. Then, from a corner of my eye, I spotted Scott Gibbs getting stuck into the grog and no doubt feeling down because he had gone over on an ankle against Border, the reason I had been called off the bench. It's funny the little doubts that run through your mind, especially so far from home. I trusted Andy Keast – but I also knew he was trying to sign me for Quins and therefore trying to build up a relationship.

Scott Gibbs, on the other hand, had absolutely nothing to gain by telling me how well I played. Quite the opposite, in fact, because I could soon be a rival for his Test slot – and a more confident rival as a consequence of him massaging my ego. It seemed, though, that Scott had already resigned himself to figuring in the midweek XV at best. At worst was the plane ticket home. Scott's tour really was at a crossroads. As I tried to cheer up the disconsolate Gibbs, I was conscious of Dai Young winking at me and saying I was odds-on to become the Test inside centre. Gibbs endorsed Young's view, saying, 'I'm struggling – but you're playing well.' I reckoned Gibbsy was down but far from out, and what he really needed was a bit of reassurance. I told him he was the man for the job at inside centre – and I couldn't have said a truer word on tour, because that's how it turned out. He was the prize guy by the time we reached journey's end. I really did mean it, too. Gibbs picked himself off the floor, almost literally, and became the Lions' 'man of the series'.

As I said earlier, Fran Cotton and Ian McGeechan were reared in rugby league country and respected our qualities as well as the fact we are out-and-out competitors from a school of hard knocks. But it was increasingly apparent to me that the top rugby union guys like Guscott had enormous skill. When Jerry opened up in training he was really quick. Like Martin Offiah, in fact, but able to use his hands and feet as well. He was so much more than a finisher.

Competition was certainly intense at centre and I was more than happy to fit in on the wing, although I had the utmost respect for Ieuan Evans. Throughout my transition back to rugby union Ieuan had been an inspiration. He's six or seven months older than me and was still playing at the top of his game. I'd played against him at international level in an earlier 'life', including the occasion when he scored an amazing try against Scotland at the Arms Park, side-stepping infield to the posts. A thoroughbred winger, he has physical strength as well as pace and skill.

My main worry was that some sections of the press were – how shall I put this? – keen for John Bentley to make the Test line-up, and maybe not for the right reasons. Call me an old cynic. But John was always so obliging with the hand-crafted quote it was hard to resist a temptation to think that it might have been partly behind the media's enthusiasm. Sure, John had scored a fabulous try against Gauteng Lions, when he carved up a bewildered defence on a mazy run from around halfway, and that score confirmed his abilities going forward. But I had every confidence in my defence being the more solid.

There was something else troubling me, though, as crunch time neared. It seemed that every time a Lion went down injured and had to be pensioned off, speculation regarding his likely successor started with a roll call of English stand-bys. I don't blame the English press for touting the guys they knew because, basically, they have to pander to their market. But whilst I recognise that fact, there were certainly a few in the media ranks who seemed to forget that they were working for national newspapers or broadcasting outlets monitored further afield than England. Every time a player had to be replaced, the call went up from the media for another Englishman to be flown out. Never mind the fact that Scotland were already touring Southern Africa with players of the calibre of Craig Chalmers, Andy Nicol and Ian Smith on hand, or that the Irish were proving the stars of our trip despite being unsung in advance. It was always an Englishman who was touted as the 'obvious' replacement.

If the press guys were only doing their job and selling papers, I have to confess I was shocked when word came back from a com-mittee formed to discuss replacements that it was a waste of time nominating Scots, Irish or Welsh candidates. My source confided, 'It's just not worth attending these meetings. It's just one Englishman after another who is being put up for consideration.' For the record, the tour replacements were Mike Catt (England), Nigel Redman (England), Tony Diprose (England), Kyran Bracken (England) and –

finally – Tony Stanger (Scotland). All fine players. But draw your own conclusions nevertheless, and I certainly didn't buy the line about English players being more battle-hardened through being in Argentina. Not when Scotland were just up the road, and when Bryan Redpath, the international scrum-half from Melrose, had proved his recovery from injury by turning out for the Barbarians in Italy.

I don't make these accusations lightly but out of genuine concern that this is an issue capable of threatening future Lions tours. There were similar worries when the Welsh were predominant in 1977, and the situation will have to be watched. Doubtless I'll be accused of driving a wedge into the solidarity of the Lions, and perhaps even of xenophobia. But I do believe that one, possibly two, countrymen received a raw deal from the '97 Lions selectors, especially when you consider that a mere five players in the original squad was Scotland's lowest representation since the Second World War.

Equally worrying was the experience being offered to so many Englishmen in the first place. It is always hard enough for the other Five Nations countries to compete because of limited resources. The fact that the English would be capable of subsequently fielding an entire team of Lions didn't help. I am just thankful for the strength of character possessed by Jim Telfer, who ensured he got the front five he wanted in the pack without being steamrollered into picking Englishmen with much-vaunted reputations. Telfer is one of the strongest and most honest characters I've come across – qualities he looks for in a player – and his ability to argue his corner was certainly needed on tour. Thanks I'm sure to him, the front five eventually nominated were very much the men in form but far removed from those generally perceived as first choices when the Lions set out. Telfer trusted his judgement in going for Tom Smith (Scotland), Keith Wood (Ireland), Paul Wallace (Ireland), Jeremy Davidson (Ireland) and Martin Johnson, our captain and the sole Englishman in that department. Let me quickly add, though, that the English back row of Lawrence Dallaglio, Tim Rodber and Richard Hill were vital to the cause.

Dallaglio was a huge influence as far as I was concerned in stopping the Springbok dangerman Gary Teichmann in his tracks. The way we planned it, Henry Honiball had to be checked in the backs, because he is one of the best ball players I have seen since Tony Myler of Widnes. Honiball could offload a pass at any time and in any situation. But, if the support runners are covered, you tend to look pretty daft. That's what happened with Dallaglio taking out Teichmann, and the big hits on the Springbok forwards coming round the side of the rucks were the key to lowering the world champions' colours. Rodber also had a massive role in that respect.

Before the Test action got under way we heard about selections by means of an envelope slipped under the bedroom door before breakfast, in my view a silly practice. I was sharing a room before the first Test in Cape Town with Will Greenwood, who knew he had missed out – unlike myself, who received a note of congratulations saying I had been selected for the squad. The trouble was I didn't know if I was in the team or set to warm the bench. The suspense was crippling, and the management added to it by trying to prevent us from discussing the subject until the official announcement. In the hotel dining-room that morning I found everybody communicating in whispers, and eventually I worked out by process of elimination that I was on the wing to face the 'Boks.

It is fair to say that the choice of yours truly on the wing did not meet with universal acclaim. I know I had the confidence of Ian McGeechan, which is what mattered. But the press reaction centred mainly on the omission of John Bentley, who, poor guy, had been up since 5.30 a.m., apparently waiting by the side of the lift on his floor of the hotel, anxious to take delivery of an envelope . . .

At the conference to announce the team, Ian McGeechan was put under considerable pressure to explain why I had got the nod. What it came down to was defensive qualities. Bentley's defence is capable, but he had been known to make some bad decisions at unfortunate times going into the Test series. That may sound rich coming from me in view of what was to happen at a crucial moment of the series later on, when I fell for one of the oldest tricks in the book. But, overall, I had confidence in my ability to put the shutters up when necessary, and I was quite happy to move from centre to wing and do my bit. The outcry surrounding the omission of Bentley did, however, provide a reminder that certain people were inclined to forget that the Lions were a composite team and not England under another guise.

So close to glory: in the 1992 Rugby League World Cup final at Wembley, I found myself held up over the Australian try-line and sandwiched between two opponents. Great Britain lost 10–6 (© Sig Kasatkin).

Wembley woe: the pain of a Challenge Cup defeat by Wigan is beginning to sink in as I trudge back to the dressing-room having collected a souvenir hat from a fan (© Dave Williams).

One of the highlights of my career was captaining Scotland in rugby league's Emerging Nations World Cup. I was very proud of our team of amateurs and students backed up by a handful of pros. We looked the part, too! (© Dave Williams)

Icing on the cake: I celebrated my return to Scotland colours after a nine-year absence playing rugby league by scoring a try against Ireland at Murrayfield, a match Scotland won 38–10. It may not look pretty but colleague Rowen Shepherd looked pleased enough and the touchdown was voted 'try of the season' in *The Herald* rugby awards (© Fotosport).

Throughout my sporting life I've been fortunate to have had help from
John Dawson (right), a sprint coach and a rugby journalist
in the Scottish Borders.

Gym'll fix it: that's me in the blue corner slugging it out with Gregor
Townsend during the British Lions tour of South Africa. I'm a great
believer that working out with boxing gloves and pads can sharpen
a player's reflexes.

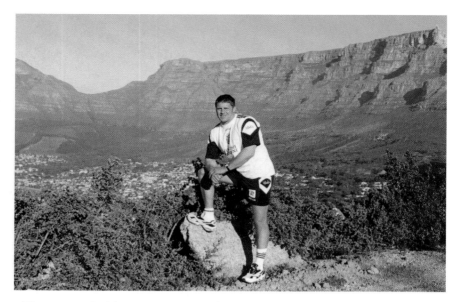

Time out at Table Mountain: a reflective moment during the Cape Town leg of the Lions tour.

Communication is vital in rugby, especially in the heat of Test-match action with the Lions against the Springboks, where the stakes don't come much higher. Here I chip in my tuppence worth (© Fotosport).

Try-time for the Lions after Springbok substitute Russell Bennett is too late to cut off my route to the clinching score in the vital first-Test victory in Cape Town. At this precise moment my thoughts were actually with my folks back home (© Fotosport).

How many times have you heard rugby players insist that they never read the papers? Caught in the act in Cape Town in 1997, after the British Lions had won the first Test against South Africa (© Fotosport).

Lift off: a Lions victory over the Springboks is secure, but there is no need to rush back to earth because it is important to savour the moment for as long as possible (© Fotosport).

A pride of Lions: (left to right) Jason Leonard, me, Scott Gibbs and John Bentley after the Test series against the world champion Springboks had been clinched in Durban.

Scots corner: Gregor Townsend, Tom Smith and yours truly fly the flag after the Test series against South Africa concluded at Ellis Park, Johannesburg. Both Gregor and I were injured and missed the 'dead' rubber (© Fotosport).

Trophies – I love 'em, as tangible evidence of achievement. Here I'm lifting the Sanyo Challenge Trophy after Newcastle boss Rob Andrew kindly asked me to captain the team on my farewell appearance, which brought victory over a World XV at Twickenham in 1998. It's important to move on with happy memories (© Fotosport).

The Tait gallery: Caroline, Michael, Me and Zoey (© Peter Kemp).

The first Test was a cliffhanger by any standards, swaying to and fro until the closing moments when I managed to collect a pass and go over in the corner for the clinching try. My return to the Scotland team had been historic on account of the fact that nobody had ever returned to pull on the dark blue jersey after playing rugby league. But as regards the number of people I knew who would share my celebrations, that try for the Lions was the ultimate. The first thing that crossed my mind after I'd dotted the ball down was a feeling of joy for my family back home and what they would be thinking. Over my shoulder I could see the squad members and back-up personnel racing off the Lions bench, punching the air with delight and spilling on to the pitch. But my inner thoughts were, even by then, several thousand miles away.

A fraction of a second after touching down, I indulged myself with a little dance of delight. I probably borrowed the idea from Martin Offiah, who was brilliant at letting his feelings out and sharing joy with the fans. But I'll never know why I suddenly decided that my fingers should be a pistol and that I should 'shoot' the crowd! The Lions nicknamed me 'Pistol Pete' and Stuart Barnes refers to my 'quasi-gun-toting celebrations' in his book *Rugby's New-Age Travellers*. There was nothing quasi about my celebration at all, Stuart. I was utterly rapt at clinching our 25–16 win. Mind you, it wasn't the sort of thing I'd have done if we had scored in the first minute, leaving them plenty of time to come back. I knew it was game, set and match to us and my gesture was more in the way of a victory salute to Lions fans who had travelled in extraordinarily large numbers.

It's not a bad thing to be remembered for scoring a Test-clinching try and celebrating wildly. The days of reacting sombrely to scoring are hopefully long gone, and as a youngster I used to marvel at how players could touch down for their country and then trot back to the halfway line as though they were late for a funeral. As I was lucky enough to discover, the stiff-upper-lip reaction is in direct contrast to how you are feeling inside. Now that rugby is professional, surely it is time to involve the crowd a bit more. I just wonder who'll be the first player to pull his shirt over his head Ravanelli-style? My money is on Richard Cockerill, the England hooker who brandished the badge on his jersey after that penalty try at Murrayfield in 1998. Gets everybody going, that does. There were some in the Scottish team who'd have had Cockerill up on a disrepute charge given half a chance were it not for the fact that they believe it will be their turn to do the same to the England fans one day.

I was as happy as a lark to learn after my Cape Town try that my grandmother, Mary Lieds, had been passing the Black Swan pub in Kelso and heard an enormous roar at the precise moment I touched the ball down. Gran said she thought the roof was going to blow away. It had to be the Black Swan, my favourite watering hole and one run by Ian Cassie, a convivial host and a rugby man. If you are ever passing by the Black Swan, drop in for a pint and see the decorations that include a selection of my jerseys on the wall. Following my return from South Africa, Ian Cassie threw a party and even commissioned a painting of me in my Lions kit.

While I was away, I gather there was some debate about whether my achievement should be recognised by the local council in my home town of Kelso. Word reached me that the subject was raised, but the feeling among councillors was that since I was playing for an English club no action should be taken. If that's the case then I'm sad. Especially when Tony Stanger, called up for the final match against Northern Free State, received good-luck faxes from the Hawick Community Council, not to mention his old school. Of course, as a former head boy Tony had longer to get to know the teachers. I was out of the door of Kelso High at the earliest possible opportunity! It is the case, though, that nearly every Lion received a message of support from his home town – except me. But what really mattered was the recognition of the regulars at the Black Swan, the friendliest pub in Scotland.

The feedback concerning reaction to my try was really reassuring too. It is one of the strange things about touring that those at the heart of the action often find it impossible to gauge the impact of their deeds. And you know what they say about feedback being the breakfast of champions! We were desperate to know how our efforts were being received beyond closest relatives, and the fact that the Lions matches were being shown only on satellite television appeared to make little difference to the profile of the tour in a summer when, admittedly, there was no major football tournament or Olympic Games.

As the dust settled on that first Test, I was so glad to have given Ian McGeechan a return for the confidence he had shown in me by opting to play me ahead of John Bentley. But to this day I remain amazed at South Africa's decision to take the opening Test of the series to a ground at sea level. That always registered as a massive own goal. I would have thought the 'Boks would have been astute enough to have taken us up to altitude at, say, Bloemfontein, where there is a magnificent stadium, if they wanted to save the last Test for Johannesburg. At international level every little advantage simply has to be seized.

Durban, venue for the second Test a week later, was also at sea level, and we approached this encounter with confidence and high expectations. By this time John Bentley had come into the side for the injured Ieuan Evans, and while it is fair to say he too had his problems, I was about to choke on some of my earlier comments about defence. John missed a simple tackle but mistakes were spread throughout the team as the 'Boks scored three tries to nil. I was caught up in the general malaise. In fact, I still can't believe how naïve I was in offloading a pass to their stand-off Henry Honiball for one of those home tries. We were inside our own twenty-two when Matt Dawson slipped a pass to me which came by surprise because I thought he'd take the ball up and create a ruck. I might have been off-guard, but that's no excuse for what happened next. The crafty Honiball simply yelled 'Yep' and, thinking the call had to be from a fellow Lion, I obligingly gave him the pass he'd asked for. Try-time to the Springboks. For a moment I was consumed by the notion that if the Lions lost that Test and then the series, it would be traced back to that single moment. And to me . . .

All praise to Neil Jenkins, who had been keeping the tryless Lions in touch with his metronomic goal-kicking. He slotted another penalty to put us level – his fifth – and by the time Jerry Guscott had slotted the winning drop goal five minutes from the end, I had retired with a groin strain. Heaven knows how much I aggravated the injury by leaping from the bench and rushing forward – out of relief as well as delight – when Guscott applied the *coup de grâce* in an 18–15 victory. It was a spontaneous reaction and not in keeping with the decision by our physio, Mark Davies, to take me off.

Proof of Mark's wisdom came when the Springboks made one final do-or-die effort, based on Honiball hoisting a wicked kick which travelled behind the Lions' try-line and took an enormous bounce.

The day was saved by my replacement, Austin Healey, who had diligently covered across to touch down and gain a drop-out from which Neil Jenkins kicked the ball dead, knowing time was up. I know I'd never have got across to retrieve the situation the way Austin did, but the real hero of the hour was Jenkins. Never have I cheered a drop-out going straight into touch, preferring to see the ball being kept alive and handled. But we'd done enough. It would have been silly to push our luck.

My groin injury had no chance of clearing up in time for the third Test at Ellis Park, but the job was done anyway. In our moment of triumph Fran Cotton asked my feelings, and I drew on my rugby league instincts to reply, 'Money's in the bank. Let's go home.' Amidst the celebrations, though, I found a quiet moment to reflect on the sad passing of my friend Jonathan Davies's wife, Karen. Karen had been ill for some time and for that reason I was able to dismiss speculation that Jonathan might join the tour as a replacement when Paul Grayson was injured. But it still came as a shock to learn she had succumbed to cancer and left behind a young family. The news was broken to me in a phone call during the build-up to the second Test, and I immediately called Caroline to tell her and ask that she pass on our condolences. Our families had been reasonably close in the Widnes days and Caroline and Karen got on well. As I said on learning of her death, 'Talk of clinching the series and giving the fans something to celebrate seems inappropriate given what Jonathan must be feeling, but we've got to do the best we can.'

Fran and a few of the lads tried to maintain that there was still a lot to play for in the third Test, but I think they knew in their hearts it was kidology. It was different perhaps in 1974, when the Lions kept the momentum going to maintain an unbeaten tour record by drawing the final Test. But that was before the onset of highly intensive domestic competition which inevitably meant the players had to pull themselves up by the bootlaces to go on tour in the first place. By the time the series was won, many of us were hanging together with the help of tape and string – no doubt to the concern of Newcastle's owner Sir John Hall, who had expressed some reservations when he had heard the club would be contributing heavily to the tour. Indeed, the Falcons were represented by myself, Tony Underwood, Doddie Weir, Tim Stimpson and John Bentley.

It is so hard to build yourself up for a 'dead' rubber, knowing the series is in the bag, but Fran did have a point when he mentioned that no Lions team had ever whitewashed South Africa in a Test series. Perhaps Fran was keener than even he thought on pay-back for his '74 team, who were denied that clean sweep by a controversial decision which denied Fergus Slattery a clinching try.

Anyway, the Springboks regained a bit of pride by winning the last Test 35–16, but I was still determined the Lions should have the last word. Tom Smith had declared that if the Springboks won they would attempt to make out that the previous two encounters had just never happened, and that was exactly the way things were shaping up. Sitting in the stand, I could see that the Springboks were trying to take the limelight away from the Lions, so I slipped into my command mode and organised an impromptu lap of honour. The gutted expressions on the faces of the home players as they looked over their shoulders during television interviews and saw us parading the trophy was something to behold. The 'Boks knew they couldn't hide from the fact that they had won a relatively meaningless skirmish, whereas to the Lions went the true prize. That really rubbed it in for the Springboks.

Celebrations were immense, and I was pleased to welcome into our midst old friends from back home in the Borders, John Dawson, Richard Fleming and Dick Allan. At the height of the partying, though, I noticed that the trophy for winning the series was missing. Nothing untoward had happened to the silverware, it was just that nobody had bothered to bring it along. As far as I was concerned this was a major oversight, since the cup symbolised our triumph. In rugby league we would always fill any trophy that came our way and drink to what had been achieved. When I mentioned this to Fran Cotton he was sympathetic to my request. He gave me the key to his room, where the trophy was 'resting', and I was back in no time, passing the silverware around. It proved to be an emotional finale and above all I enjoyed the opportunity the Lions provided to work with professionals.

It was indeed strange to think that Scott Gibbs and Allan Bateman had been bitter rivals at one point in my career but were now my closest allies. I also made some good friends from outside the rugby league circle, including reserve hooker Barry Williams from Wales and Eric Miller from Ireland. Eric was on the field at the dénouement in Durban and I felt he was unfortunate not to have played a bigger part in the overall triumph. I believe he had actually been chosen ahead of Tim Rodber but a late change of policy had robbed him of his place. The Lions officials even tried to make out that Eric had flu in justifying the alteration to the line-up. Not so.

By and large, though, the selections couldn't really be faulted, and with hindsight it was interesting to see where the management had come from with some of their picks. For instance, Lawrence Dallaglio, Richard Hill and Martin Johnson were out-and-out winners in my estimation, more than any other players on the tour. Then again everybody who went to South Africa was a winner, but how the selectors recognised those qualities so far in advance was a gift on their part. Whether they could see it on the field or whether it was by chance, the blend was such that everybody was fighting for the same cause.

What intrigued me a bit was to see some players long after the tour was over still trying to milk their Lions fame and building their rugby reputation around what had happened in three months. I feel I achieved more playing rugby league, and playing for Scotland is something else I wouldn't trade for a Lions tour. Fran, though, was generous about my contribution in his book *My Pride of Lions*. He wrote, 'Alan was the consummate professional. He never stopped working on his game and he was the type to always do extra work in the gym. He was taken as a utility player, covering various positions, and he had a bloody good tour all round.'

You can't say fairer than that! I was grateful to him for his words, and also to the fan who passed down to me a scarf as I sat on the Lions replacements' bench out in South Africa during one of the early skirmishes. I didn't pay too much attention at first. Then I realised it was a special scarf. In fact it was a Kelso scarf, which went on to become my lucky mascot on the journeys between Witbank, Welkom and Wellington, and so on. Even thousands of miles away from home, that scarf made me feel I was still attached to my roots.

CHAPTER EIGHT

Worlds Apart

England might have expected. But I was never the man to deliver for them, no matter how hard they tried to get me into their rugby league jersey to face Wales back in 1995. I have to confess that, initially at least, I was flattered to receive a letter offering me a place in the England side, since the fixture with the Welsh opened up a route to the World Cup that was being played later that year as part of centenary celebrations. But then Wales protested about my eligibility, which started me thinking – and worrying about how I could look my friends and family in the eye.

The rule book did indeed state that even though I was born in Scotland I qualified to uphold the honour of St George on the grounds that I had played my first game of rugby league in England. But some things, you are aware deep down, can never be. Knowing the thrill I got from pulling on the Scottish rugby union shirt, my conscience just would not have allowed me to do anything that would, inevitably, have devalued that achievement. I couldn't have lived with people saying, 'Oh, look, there's Alan Tait – he'll play international rugby for anybody, provided the fee is right.'

The same thoughts, I'm sure, must have preoccupied Ian McGeechan when England made a formal approach to him to be their coach early in the 1997–98 season. In theory there was nothing to stop Geech taking up the challenge, especially in a professional game where individuals have to do the best for themselves and their families. And, let's face it, England's vast resources make them far likelier World Cup winners than Scotland. That, though, is to ignore the emotional reality. How could Geech have looked at himself in the mirror on the morning of a Calcutta Cup match at Murrayfield? The highlight of my sporting life was being capped by Scotland for the first time at the 1987 rugby union World Cup. After that my greatest moment was undoubtedly running out at Murrayfield. To have worn the England kit would have taken the shine off some amazing memories – and left me wide open to charges of being a rugby mercenary. I would have been cheating myself and also an up-and-coming English youngster desperate for the honour. Besides, I reckoned I was only a few years away from moving back to live in Scotland – the bungalow was in the process of being built outside Kelso – and I'd have run the risk of being branded locally as a bit of a joke.

The practical solution was to retire completely from international rugby after a 14-Test career, because England were *de facto* Great Britain, with a few notable exceptions. If I refused to represent England then the coaches would take it to mean that I was no longer ambitious for representative honours and would leave me out of their long-term plans. In fact, though, I was still ambitious in the right circumstances, and there was nothing more tempting for me than the chance to play for Scotland in the Emerging Nations World Cup, which was due to run parallel with the main event. All right, the standard would be much lower. But I would be more comfortable helping Scotland than a cause which – no disrespect intended – was alien to me.

There was just one snag, however. Scotland were having bother convincing the rugby league authorities that they would be strong enough even for the minor event. That the battle was eventually won is a tribute to the persistence of Carlisle secretary Paul Scanlon-Wells, a Scot who circulated every top rugby league club appealing for players with a suitable qualification to come forward. Players of the calibre of Halifax's Martin Ketteridge, London Bronco Darren Shaw and Huddersfield's Darrall Shelford were unearthed, each of them boasting Scottish ancestry. In addition, Hugh Waddell, the Carlisle forward, had a useful rugby league pedigree, as did the Maori Charlie McAllister, one of several players drawn from the amateur ranks. Hugh had represented Great Britain whilst at the Oldham club, while Charlie was one of the characters of the squad, having qualified through a grandfather born in the Mull of Kintyre who had joined the navy as a young man. Apparently Charlie's grandad then got caught up in a mutiny off New Zealand and jumped ship before going into hiding. When a royal pardon was eventually issued, grandfather McAllister stayed on and married a Maori girl, with far-reaching consequences for Scottish rugby league! The remainder of the 21-man squad comprised students.

I was delighted to receive an invitation to take on the captaincy extended by manager John Risman, a former Fulham professional. A member of one of rugby league's most famous families – father Gus captained Great Britain, while brother Bev was a dual international – John, a driving force in Scottish Students rugby league, explained that coaching would be shared between my Kelso predecessor George Fairbairn and Keith Davies, a stalwart of Cumbrian rugby league. In addition to the challenge of trying to give rugby league a profile in Scotland, it occurred to me that I'd be getting three weeks away from the Leeds club, where I wasn't exactly the first name coach Dean Bell put down on his team-sheet.

George Fairbairn and I quickly embarked on some serious planning and agreed it would be helpful to have a training weekend where players could actually get to know each other. Kelso was an obvious, if sentimental, choice of base for both of us, and so members of the squad were booked into a local hotel on a Saturday morning and were soon out on the training pitch. I have to confess to being shocked by the modest standard, even the most elementary drills proving a major challenge for some. But George prevailed upon me to withhold judgement, which was sound advice.

Come the first match, against a Russian side who had actually beaten a French Division One outfit during their build-up, every one of our students and amateurs put their bodies on the line in a manner which astounded me. Maybe it was the way management had appealed to the players' sense of heritage by acquiring kilts for the entire squad. Or the fact that a piper was in attendance as we ran out on to Featherstone's Post Office Road ground. But we surpassed ourselves in a famous 34–9 victory, helped by an outstanding display from the hitherto unknown Loughborough University winger Alisdair Blee, who deservedly won the man-of-the-match award.

The Scotland rugby leaguers were up and running, and the next time out we defeated USA 36–16 at Northampton in a match which hung in the balance for a long spell and eventually boiled down to who wanted victory more. That left us needing to overcome the Cook Islands at Castleford for the right to a place in the final at Bury Football Club's Gigg Lane ground. My Leeds colleague Kevin Iro hailed from the Cook Islands and he told me how seriously they took the game in that part of the world. Suitably briefed, I confided to George Fairbairn that we'd do well to keep the margin within 20 points, but at half-time we were actually leading. Had the ball not been dropped over the opposition line at a critical stage an upset could well have been on the cards, but, alas, there was to be no fairytale ending as we went down 20–10.

It may sound corny, but captaining that Scotland rugby league side was a magical experience, and my only disappointment was that no match was arranged on home soil. If, say, we had been delegated to play in the Borders, the impact would have been even greater and might have generated the inspiration we needed to reach the final. As things stood, though, the Scottish performance overall was the catalyst for an amateur competition to spring up north of the border, helped also by a 26–6 victory over Ireland at Partick Thistle FC, a match in which I flagged up my desire to return to rugby union.

That clash with the tiny Cook Islands unlocked fond memories of one of my strangest ever international assignments with Great Britain five years earlier. We were *en route* to play New Zealand and stopped off for a two-Test series in Papua New Guinea, the only rugby destination where I have been seriously worried for my safety. I'd read beforehand that PNG contained some of the world's most primitive people, renowned for Stone Age cultures, and isolated tribes were being discovered up until fairly recently. I saw no evidence of cannibalism, but what I did discover was that this beautiful land possessed the most fanatical supporters I have ever encountered. On arrival we were told not to venture out alone from the hotel which was to be the team's base for three weeks. The positive side of spending so long in potentially hostile surroundings was to use 100 per cent humidity to help us get fit to face the Kiwis.

The first of our five matches passed peacefully, and I watched from the sidelines as we cruised home 40–18 against South Zone in Port Moresby. It was on leaving the capital to travel up country to Lae that the fireworks began. The first surprise came when, following an internal flight, we were obliged to walk from the airport to our hotel carrying our own bags. In the steamy heat, sweat flowed from us in rivers.

The locals, at this stage, could not have been friendlier, singing and cheering as we made our way up the road. By contrast, the journey to the ground was a terrifying experience, with fans banging on the side of the bus and making threatening gestures. A couple of times I thought we were dead meat, and coach Mal Reilly insisted that the bus keep going through the milling crowds, issuing instructions that on no account were we to stop. Once at the rustic little 'stadium', there seemed to be ten times more people outside than inside, and the pitch was a nightmare – rough volcanic stone interspersed with grassy patches. In fact the authorities had ordered the gates to be locked when the ground was full to overflowing, a decision which prompted those unable to gain entry or denied access to surrounding trees to start stoning the entrances. Some of our players were hailed as heroes by the travelling press for rescuing female turnstile attendants. When order was restored, Great Britain went on to win 24–10.

These disturbances merely prepared us for even greater trouble when travelling on to Garoka for the first Test, where I made my tour entrance at full-back. Again there were too many people for the small venue, inside which the atmosphere was truly intimidating. Away from the games the crowds just wanted to express their enthusiasm; in a game environment they would whip themselves up into a frenzy. With bottles and other assorted debris being hurled on to the pitch, the referee halted play after approximately 15 minutes, and I remember rifle shots being fired into the air and tear-gas being sprayed on sections of the packed terracing. When play eventually resumed, our knees were cut to shreds on the stony surface, and to add to our discomfort it seemed as though every decision went against us. In the circumstances, 20–18 was a reasonably respectable margin of defeat, and my abiding memory is of contesting a decision, to be asked by the ref, 'Do you want to get out of here alive?'

But for disallowed tries we would undoubtedly have won, but problems didn't end there. Having seen Papua New Guinea achieve what was hailed as one of their greatest results, home supporters decided they'd like a few souvenirs. For an hour afterwards players and officials alike formed a circle to protect our kit and medical supplies. Not that this deterred the fans in their quest for souvenirs. At one hotel locals got into the compound and swiped players' kit that was hanging out to dry on the verandah. It was quite a sight the following day to see some of our hosts running around, quite unabashed, playing rugby league wearing Great Britain jerseys!

The island was rocking during our visit as a consequence of that win by the Kabuls, as the PNG side are called, and even more fans turned up to see our match against another Zonal Select at Rabaul in the tropical paradise of New Britain. Great Britain eventually won 50–4 but chaos reigned once more and tear-gas fired at the terracing drifted across the pitch, causing players to flee with towels wrapped around their heads. As a sequel to the troubles, the local police chief was thrown into gaol for prematurely ordering guards to fire off the gas canisters.

Port Moresby, where we'd been warned not to leave the hotel, seemed like an ocean of tranquillity when we returned and, drawing confidence from the fence which surrounded the country's main pitch, we banished memories of the first Test defeat to win 40–8.

Not content with a Test win, the Papua New Guineans also wanted a larger share of the gate receipts. At least that's how it appeared to our manager Maurice Lindsay, a former bookmaker and always the shrewdest of operators where money was concerned. Stretching his managerial powers to the limit, Maurice requisitioned a couple of players to act as minders as he visited the various points of entry to claim our share of the spoils at source. Once delivered, the cash was deposited in a large sack slung over Maurice's shoulder. For obvious reasons, none of the players were keen to 'ride shotgun' voluntarily, but Maurice press-ganged them in the knowledge that if he waited until the following day for the money we would never have got our share. I treasure the memory of Maurice carrying his sack and setting out on his rounds. He would have made a lovely Santa Claus.

Although there were incidents on that leg of the trip which left me frightened, I have mainly happy memories of Papua New Guinea, summed up by an incident which occurred on our five-mile journey from a game back to our hotel at the end of the tour. Several of the players were throwing items of kit to the crowds from the bus and I got into the spirit by lobbing an old pair of boots out of the window. Several hours later I was resting in my room when I answered a knock on my door to find a local man with my boots tied together by the laces and lodged around his neck. Despite the fact that his only mode of transport was Shanks's pony, the fan had gone to the trouble of learning who I was and then coming to deliver thanks in person. What made his journey all the more remarkable was that I take size nine boots and his feet must have been size fifteen, so there wasn't the remotest chance of the footwear fitting! Clearly it was the thought that counted, as far as this grateful fan was concerned.

If only relations between myself and the Great Britain management had been on the same level as those with the recipient of my boots. Alas, it was all downhill from there on. I'd injured my groin early in the trip and didn't know what was wrong. I only knew that the pain could be quite severe. Indeed, I had to roll out of bed in the morning, and with the tour doctor reluctant to dispense anti-inflammatory tablets, my main source of relief was a few beers in the evening. The Great Britain bosses urged me to play one more match to help them through an injury crisis, and I took the view that having soldiered this far another 80 minutes would make no difference.

However, Doug Laughton noted the team selection on Teletext back home and was straight on the phone, ordering me to confront Maurice Lindsay and Mal Reilly, telling them I'd be putting myself at long-term risk. What I hadn't realised was that bad blood existed between Reilly and Widnes, stemming from the fact that he'd had his jaw broken against them in a club fixture several years before. Reilly said he expected such a lack of co-operation from Laughton, and it seemed to me I had a bit of bother getting back into the Great Britain set-up from that moment onwards. Indeed, I heard from a high-placed source that Maurice Lindsay recommended I should not be taken on tour again. On returning home I was sent to Harley Street specialist Gerry Gilmore and became one of the first diagnosed cases of a condition which has been given the name of that surgeon.

Things weren't always that bad between me and Great Britain officials, though, because I'd only been in rugby league eight months when Doug Laughton received a call from Mal Reilly asking if I had what was required at international level. Doug assured him that as far as he was concerned I was the modern-day Test full-back, with pace to burn and an eye for a gap. When regular last line Steve Hampson, from Wigan, then dropped out of the Great Britain team with a hip injury on the Wednesday prior to a Test with France, I found myself called up and charged with justifying Doug Laughton's splendid endorsement.

To say my Great Britain début went well would be a considerable understatement, as I collected the man-of-the-match award during our 26–10 victory at Central Park, Wigan. John Whalley wrote in the *Daily Telegraph*, 'The most positive factor was the confirmation that Alan Tait can make as big an impact as a professional international as he did for Scotland on the rugby union field. The arrival of Jonathan Davies at Widnes has taken much of the attention away from Tait but there is little doubt the full-back's stunning progress in only ten months is one of the biggest bonuses for Mr Reilly this season. Tait did not impress in the recent John Player Trophy final against Wigan but he clearly demonstrated his ability to handle the big occasion in his Test début. Composed and authoritative, he was Britain's best player.'

Paul Harrison told readers of *The Sun*, 'Alan Tait, the former Scottish rugby union star, launched his new international career in sizzling style at Wigan.' David Burke of the *Daily Express* maintained, 'Alan Tait launched his new international career in style as Great Britain celebrated a record-equalling seventh successive rugby league Test victory over travel-sad France at Central Park, Wigan. Classy Tait landed the man-of-the-match award as revitalised France, without a win on British soil for 22 years, failed to break their jinx despite an impressive show. Twelve months ago Tait was a key figure in Scotland's rugby union plans, but the former Kelso centre could not have made a more competent début in the international rugby league arena.' A number of papers, incidentally, noted my satisfaction that Scotland had managed a 23–7 victory over Wales in the Five Nations Championship that same day.

Our success against France provided a springboard into the Great Britain squad for a three-Test series later in 1989 against New Zealand, where, I am ashamed to say, I dropped out of the middle encounter due to injuries sustained on the dance floor! Following the first Test defeat at Old Trafford, the team were staying at Wigan in preparation for the following weekend's clash at Elland Road. Contrary to my better judgement I allowed myself to be lured on to a trip into Manchester in the company of Shaun Edwards and Martin

Offiah, who was showing off a new BMW car. The intention had been to pick up a burger, but before I knew it Martin and Shaun were convincing each other it would be a noble gesture to visit the popular Hacienda night-club. Clubbing was the last thing on my mind. Alas, there was little alternative but to go with the flow, on the understanding that we were only dropping in for approximately half an hour.

Both Martin and Shaun were into rave music in a big way, and rather than hang around in the shadows I joined in the spirit of the evening and was soon in the midst of hundreds of revellers jumping up and down and blowing whistles. At 2 a.m. we were still in the Hacienda, and when you sweat in such places you really sweat. I must have spent three hours bouncing up and down on the spot before Martin and Shaun dragged me back to the Great Britain team hotel. On the return journey my legs seized up and I was engulfed by stiffness; the following morning, a Thursday, I pulled a hamstring in training. The explanation was obvious: I had dehydrated myself and my muscles had rebelled at heavy exercise before fluid I'd lost had been replenished. Having just got into the Great Britain team I had gifted Steve Hampson his place straight back. It was a lesson well and truly learned.

Maybe Great Britain honours had come just a little too easy for me anyway, if I could have been so easily talked into breaking camp. While other aspirants are required to graft and toil for years, I'd found myself in the GB set-up within a year of switching from rugby union. And, yet, by the same token, there would be plenty of occasions in the years ahead when I would be on the outside of the Great Britain side looking in and desperate to play. This was never more so than when Ellery Hanley got the job of Great Britain coach for the 1994 Test series with the Australian Kangaroos. I felt I had an outstanding chance of selection because as a Leeds club-mate of Hanley's I had a chance to impress the boss every week. I knew I was playing well, but come the first Test at Wembley Ellery opted for Jonathan Davies at full-back. I was gutted but never said much. Nor could I have any legitimate grounds for complaint when Great Britain won – despite finishing with 12 men after Shaun Edwards had been sent off – and Jonathan scored a marvellous long-range try.

However, a dislocated shoulder forced Jonathan out of the squad for the second Test at Old Trafford and I sat in anticipation of a call that would put me in a position to help clinch a series and rewrite part of rugby league history. Alas, that call went instead to Graham Steadman. Bristling with indignation, I rounded on Ellery and asked what was wrong. As if I didn't know. My mind went back four years to that Great Britain tour when I'd baled out injured but not before I'd turned down a request to help the team out by playing in one final match. Was I paranoid about the selection process? Ellery indicated that my absence was down to a conversation he'd had with the Wigan contingent who had advised him they would prefer a full-back with a more prodigious boot than I had. Yet, as far as I was concerned, the ability to kick 'downtown' had gone out of the game.

I deliberately watched the second Test to see how often Graham Steadman kicked and noted in dismay that he did so only twice. And yet I had been assured that this was the decisive factor in his selection ahead of me. When I challenged Hanley he began to suggest, for the first time, that there might have been politics involved. Not that it really mattered. There wasn't a lot I could do if the powers that be didn't want me.

As fate would have it, Great Britain were disrupted by the need for a further change at full-back when Graham Steadman dropped out of the deciding third Test. But my card had been well and truly marked and my fall-out years earlier surely had to be the reason, especially considering that the weekend before that decisive Test Leeds were in action at Workington and I scored two tries, including an 80-yarder. The Leeds supporters in the crowd started chanting 'Tait for Britain' and 'Are you watching, Ell-er-ee?'. I'm convinced Hanley knew I was the man for the job at that stage but his hands were tied. Forces were at work in the background and these same characters decreed that Gary Connolly should be moved from centre to full-back rather than draft me in. I was devastated. But what did I expect? My face had never really fitted, and it saddened me to realise that if I had played just one more Test for Great Britain I'd have finished my league career alongside Dave Valentine as the second most capped Scot. As it was I finished three short of George Fairbairn's record 17 Tests for a Scottish rugby league player.

Despite being snubbed so often, I had still managed to come within six inches of giving rugby league its greatest cause for celebration. Roughly the width of this page. That's how close I came to snatching a try which could have proved to be the winner against Australia in a World Cup final at Wembley. Let me explain that World Cups in rugby league are rather different from the rugby union version. With so few countries capable of competing at international level in league, the format governing the 1992 tournament was based on results of tour matches during the preceding four years. It was a long and winding road for one crunch game at Wembley, although the occasion was still a massive one.

Between embarking on the qualifying and reaching the World Cup final, I had switched from Widnes to Leeds and struck a sufficiently good patch of form for coach Mal Reilly to bring me back into the squad. For the final I was named as substitute, but Joe Lydon was struggling with a hamstring injury and for most of the week's training had taken part with his leg heavily strapped. At the last workout before the game Joe again wore a heavy bandage and confided to me back in the dressing-room that there was no way he'd finish the final. Joe was probably not being thoroughly professional by looking to start, but he knew he would last for a while before that hamstring went and I suppose it was good of him to tip me the wink, because when you are in line to face opposition containing outstanding players of the calibre of Mal Meninga, Glen Lazarus and Bradley Clyde you have to be properly prepared.

Joe did indeed start the final and there were a couple of incidents where he might have been able to make a telling break had he not been concerned about the prospect of the hamstring snapping. In fact, I could tell Joe was struggling by half-time, so I was surprised he went back out after the interval. Within eight minutes of the restart, however, his hamstring went and I was on in a World Cup final with Great Britain attacking the Aussie line. We called a move which required Martin Offiah to take the ball from our stand-off at a scrum with me in support. In training Martin had chosen to accept the tackle and play the ball through his legs, but this time he chose to offload a pass in contact to me. I never thought for a moment that Martin would pass and just wasn't ready. Had I been more aware and adjusted to the pace of the game then I might have taken the pass and scored, because a massive gap yawned open in front of me. Instead I knocked on and the fact that the mistake occurred on the first tackle left me wishing the ground could have opened up and swallowed me.

I chided myself at making such an awful start to the biggest match of my career, but I settled down after that and was helped by catching an awkward high ball. The game was evenly poised and time was running out when Ellery Hanley called on Shaun Edwards to put up a high, hanging kick, once known as an up-and-under but latterly labelled 'the bomb', to pressurise the Aussie full-back, Tim Brasher. Immediately the ball was airborne I took off across the turf, aiming to be directly underneath it when it descended, and more in hope than expectation I leapt, aiming to make a deflection. To my astonishment I found the ball stuck to the palm of my hand as if by glue. The next thing I knew I had pulled the ball into my body, and I was heading over the Australian line under their posts when progress was abruptly halted by Brasher. I struggled to get the ball down but it was lodged between Brasher, his colleague, Steve Renouf, and myself, with the referee, positioned five yards away, appearing to sympathise with my plight. I caught the ref's eye and he shrugged, as if to say, 'Well, do something.' Perhaps the ref had reached the stage where he wanted the game to be decided by something other than penalties and was giving me a vital split second to ground the ball and claim the try. But Brasher was hanging on to the ball as though his life depended on it and I couldn't do anything to shift him.

Ellery Hanley was right behind me and if he had fallen on top of me perhaps the ball might have been dislodged. That would have been game, set and World Cup to Great Britain, at 10–4 ahead with the conversion certain to follow. Instead Australia worked their way up to our end and came away with a clinching try when Renouf managed to get outside John Devereux, the former Welsh rugby union international and British Lion who, like me, had come on as a sub and was probably not fully attuned. Devereux, poor guy, was accused of the old rugby union failing of ball-watching rather than putting in the tackle, and a lot of flak was aimed in his direction afterwards. But it struck me – and I'm sure it occurred to Mal Reilly as well – that a former rugby union player had failed to clinch the match. And a former rugby union player had handed the opposition the initiative at the other end.

Regardless of where any blame lay, I knew that my dream of

winning at Wembley and going up those steps to collect a cup had been put on hold. At least there was satisfaction from restricting a great Kangaroos team to 10–6. No mean feat. And how many Scots have appeared in a World Cup final at any sport?

My international rugby union career had actually begun in a World Cup with a trip to the inaugural tournament in New Zealand back in 1987, where I certainly made the most of the opportunity. Listed as a replacement for the opening match against France, partly on account of Scott Hastings being injured at the first training session after our arrival, I found myself in the thick of the action after only seven minutes. In a major upheaval, our back line had to be recast following cruciate knee ligament damage to John Rutherford which effectively ended that great stand-off's career. Scotland went on to draw a pulsating match 20–20 but only after France had notched a highly contentious score when their full-back, Serge Blanco, was allowed to take a quick tap penalty and break clear while we stood around expecting the referee to allow the medics on to attend to our injured winger, Matt Duncan.

Before the thrill of that first cap had subsided I was brought back to earth by colleagues who suggested I might have broken a pre-arranged plan by rushing on to the pitch to replace Rutherford. There was a school of thought which suggested that while Dougie Wyllie moved in to stand-off, Gavin Hastings ought to have ventured up from full-back to centre with Peter Dods coming off the bench instead of me. Whether by accident or design, though, I had got my cap, and one of the men who could have verified whether or not I jumped the gun, the then Scotland manager Bob Munro, has sadly now died.

It seemed, too, that I had a chance to make the centre position mine for the duration of the tournament and initial reviews were certainly favourable. Bill McMurtrie recorded my début for *The Herald*, saying, 'Tait played a notable part in the draw that Scotland achieved. His tackling was particularly positive. With his pace and his well-made frame, almost 13 stone, he had the ability to make tackles on his terms. One on Sella not only thwarted a French attempt to run out but almost created a scoring chance for Scotland early in the second half. If Tait's fellow centre Keith Robertson had been able to take it, Scotland would have been comfortably and comfortingly more than two maximum scores ahead.' Norman Mair said in *The Scotsman*, 'Alan Tait exploded on to the scene with a physical relish that must have taken the French aback. His strength and pace were soon in evidence, not least when he held the ball up in the tackle for the support to arrive.' Alasdair Ross of *The Sun* was more succinct, remarking, 'Alan Tait had a storming game after coming on as Rutherford's replacement.'

Next up were Zimbabwe at Wellington, and I recorded my first international points from two tries in a 60–21 rout which left us facing Romania in Dunedin to round off the group. The Romanians presented no difficulties and I again claimed a brace of touchdowns in a 55–28 win, but because we had been outscored in try terms by France, a clash with the hosts, New Zealand, loomed. Record books show that we went down 30–3 in what they generously described as their toughest match of the tournament, but my memory is of being handed a few lessons by the veteran centre Joe Stanley, albeit lessons which were to stand me in good stead for the rest of my career. Basically I stood off Stanley and allowed him to run through me. From then on I was determined to be in the opposition's face at all times. I'm convinced that's the only way to take on teams like the All Blacks, and, sadly, I have to confess that not all my colleagues at that first World Cup had the proper attitude.

Soon after the showdown with the host nation had materialised, I was watching a video of the 1983 series between the All Blacks and the British Lions in the company of an established Scottish international. Noting how my Kelso team-mate Roger Baird had bounced off an All Black while attempting to make a tackle, I let out a muffled laugh. This was in no way meant as derogatory towards Roger, whose bravery in the challenge rendered him very much the worse for wear. There was just something about the way he fell that was out of the ordinary, and my 'Did you see that?' was not meant to be taken as a criticism. Unfortunately the remark was misinterpreted as mocking a fellow player, which was anything but the intention. 'Well, Pidge,' I was told. 'Instead of laughing, let's just see how you get on against them, wise guy.'

Momentarily my pride was hurt. But when I got to thinking about the way I was rebuked I came to the conclusion that it was sad that such an experienced Scotland player could be guilty of putting the opposition on so high a pedestal. I've no intention of naming the player involved but I mention the incident to emphasise the need for the mental approach to be spot on, otherwise future teams who face the All Blacks are wasting their time. The player who shot me down was a forward of considerable physical stature. Yet there he was almost shitting himself before he was due to take up a challenge. He was telling me All Blacks do this, All Blacks do that. Sure, the All Blacks were an awesome team, and they went on to win the World Cup. I respect them absolutely for that. But my colleague's attitude seemed to indicate that he was beaten before we had even started our quarter-final encounter.

Three years later I was reminded of the episode on returning to New Zealand with the Great Britain rugby league guys. We took a young side after a lot of the old heads pulled out, saying they had been there, seen it, done it. The fact that the tour didn't include Australia meant that it wasn't worth bothering about, in their view. At least that's the way it seemed, although others were genuinely recovering from a long, hard domestic season.

Whatever the reasons for the withdrawals, in the absence of the Andy Goodways, Ellery Hanleys and Andy Gregorys we took a lot of up-and-coming players. I vividly remember a lad called Ian Smailes of Featherstone Rovers who had no front teeth and was only 19 or 20 at the time of the trip. Boy, did Ian have attitude. That GB party had only just arrived in the land of the long, white cloud when a team-talk was called and somebody was trying to tell us how big and strong the Kiwis were, particularly the Iro brothers. Young Smailes chipped in, saying, 'Let's just get on the field and knock f**k out of them.' I looked into his eyes. He wasn't even a Test player, just a young kid brought along for the experience, and he never did get a Test cap. But if Smailes had been needed on our tour against the Kiwis he'd have gone on with not an ounce of fear or apprehension, and I can't say the same of everyone I've toured with on that side of the world.

If you think the All Blacks are hard men, though, what about the Papua New Guinean I encountered playing rugby league for Cumbria? In making a tackle I got hold of the lad by a part of his anatomy I later discovered was his genitalia and wrenched so hard I could feel my fingernails breaking through his skin. Later the

Cumbria team doctor came into our dressing-room and told us with a grimace of an injury which had befallen one of the opposition. Evidently I had ripped the skin right off the poor guy's penis and effectively performed a circumcision. I hope he doesn't read this and come looking for revenge!

CHAPTER NINE

Bonnie and Clyde

If there was another sport I would really like to have excelled at, unquestionably it would be sprinting. My appetite was whetted years ago when I was timed at 11.0 seconds for 100 metres on a rough grass track while preparing for a race on the summer professional athletics circuit which preoccupies many sports-minded folk in the Scottish Borders until the rugby season rolls around again. Professional athletics has long been a tradition in my native patch and – don't ask me why – the amateur version never really gets much of a look in.

Sprinting was reasonably compatible with rugby and there were definite advantages to be gained in the longer races, where the practice of running in lanes was scrapped because it did not fit in with handicapping arrangements. As competitors hurtled into the bends my upper-body strength would come in especially useful for elbowing opponents aside. I had also cultivated a reasonably powerful hand-off, but with some rivals in their fifties and even their sixties there were times when I sparked a considerable amount of booing. Maybe I was lucky to avoid becoming the first sprinter ever to be yellow-carded!

The downside of being a rugby player/sprinter was that I always carried a few extra protective pounds, which meant I could never hone down to my best weight. Also, that blue riband of the professional running circuit, the annual New Year Festival meeting in Edinburgh, fell slap bang in the middle of the rugby season. There was no way I could have peaked for such an event and maintained representative aspirations in rugby union prior to joining Widnes rugby league club. I'd love to have competed in the gala formerly known as the Powderhall Sprint, which is something Caroline has over me. We actually met through our mutual interest in running and

I told her straightaway that if we were to have a serious relationship she had better be prepared for me moving to England to play rugby league. Caroline competed twice in the New Year Festival – and caused a few ripples by complaining about her draw on the second occasion. Imagine a member of the Tait family feeling disgruntled about a sporting matter . . . Incredible! Among four women chasing the coveted sprint crown that year, Caroline was drawn in the same heat as female rival Eileen McRoberts as well as defending champion Kipper Bell from San Diego, and that didn't go down well. Indeed, Caroline told the *Daily Express*, 'I think it is a bit unfair that there is seeding for Americans and no seeding for the girls. After all, there are only four of us entered and it is hard that Eileen and I have to run against each other and Kipper Bell.'

To be fair, Caroline also admitted with a smile that taking part was the main thing as far as she was concerned. 'I ran last time and was knocked out in the heats,' she said, adding, 'I suppose the same thing will happen again.' My missus is too modest by far – as I know to my cost. One race in which she got the better of me occurred at the village of Innerleithen. I was off a handicap of 8.5 metres and she was off 21 metres. It was a credit to the handicapper that we went over the finishing line side-by-side. But a decision had to be made and Caroline got the verdict. A 'nipple finish' was the memorable description applied by Dad, always supportive of our respective running careers and invariably able to twist the arm of local butcher, Happy Wilson, for a few choice cuts of meat all in the name of sponsorship.

For some reason professional runners were able to compete for cash prizes without jeopardising their amateur status in other sports, including rugby union. Such an arrangement seemed particularly anomalous given the fact that rugby league rightly cultivated its own identity – just like athletics. Remember, too, poor Adrian Spencer, who was banned from union for playing, unpaid, in an inter-university rugby league match. That's just the way it was, though, not so very long ago in the wacky world of rugby union.

Then there was the money that could be made in professional athletics through betting, and here I have to confess that the rugby union authorities did have a point – the involvement of money was liable to cause corruption. It was never in my nature to throw a race because I had bet on another runner or to lengthen my own odds for a forthcoming event. And I never did. But plenty of runners do 'take a dive' on the professional circuit, even if the only evidence you'll find is anecdotal. Given the cash element, the handicapper always has to be an upright citizen equivalent to a steward of the Jockey Club. Spotting dodges aimed at enhancing winning prospects is a large part of his job. One occasion where the finger was unjustly pointed at me came after I had pipped Caroline to win the 1985 Lauder Games 110 metres title. Caroline finished fourth in that final but came across at the finish and gave me a warm hug. Ossie Sword, the handicapper, was shocked at our familiarity and presumed the embrace was linked to Caroline having money on me to win. Some people have cynical minds to suspect such a carve-up, I must say. True love was merely taking its course – and, naturally, Caroline knew the £250 would come in useful, especially with our wedding set for the following March! Nevertheless, Ossie, to cover himself against any subsequent outcry and mindful of the sport's desire to at least be seen to be whiter than white, penalised Caroline by adding half a metre to her handicap.

The following day the circuit moved on to Prestonpans, near Edinburgh, where Caroline, fuming at her half-metre punishment, responded by capturing the 200 metres title. I added the Tam Tait Gold Medal to the Murray Cup gained 24 hours earlier. More importantly, our combined earnings for that one weekend on the track were £580 – enough for a bathroom suite and a few bags of plaster to further assist with the flat we were doing up! In one summer alone Caroline and I netted more than £1,000 – little wonder we were known as the Bonnie and Clyde of the professional running scene.

That win at Prestonpans, incidentally, qualified me to compete in the Powderhall Classic, not to be confused with the annual New Year Sprint which brings entries from across the world. A £1,000 first prize was at stake for a sprint organised in conjunction with a greyhound meeting, and I was halfway to the bank to deposit the cheque when I was recalled for a false start in the final. It was a strange infringement, though, because the recall wasn't signalled by the starter but by a marshal who ran on to the track halfway down, waving a flag. According to the rules, that official had every right to interrupt proceedings if he felt there had been a miscarriage of justice. But he wasn't best placed to do so. I was flying that first time we got away, and I've always wondered how much my recall had to do with the fact that the marshal who flagged me came from Jedburgh which, on the rugby field at least, was a big rival of my Kelso club! In professional athletics, false starts are penalised not by disqualification but by a further handicap of a metre per infringement. Desperate for a flying start to compensate for my penalty, I promptly jumped the gun a second time and effectively ruined any prospect of Powderhall glory.

John Dawson, the trainer who launched me on the running circuit, is convinced that if I'd packed in rugby and lost half a stone but continued to work as a roofer I could have become a 100-metre sprinter in the 10.8 seconds class. Some way off being able to threaten Linford Christie, I admit. But with full-time training and better facilities, who knows how much faster I could have run? There was never any danger of athletics taking over from rugby, but I did meet some great people and the deeper I got into running the more I regarded George McNeill, a former Powderhall champion, as a hero. Even when past the 40-year-old mark George was still in tremendous shape. I remember him making introductions over the public address system at a meeting and referring to me as a lad who 'would play for Scotland at rugby one day'. Coming from someone I respected so much, that gave me a tremendous fillip. On the other hand, maybe that was George's way of telling me not to adjust my sporting priorities!

I also learned a bit from running about psyching out opponents. One of my stablemates was a guy called John Hughes, who was normally as quiet as a mouse. It was so out of character when, as I was about to settle into my blocks for a race, John walked up and said, 'You'll never see the way I go.' 'Sledging', as the Aussies call it, goes on all the time in rugby league, but that put-down from somebody I reckoned I knew well was a new and disturbing experience for me. I was so determined to make John eat his words and so amazed at his sudden bravado that I fluffed my start. On the other hand, I never did find out if John Dawson had merely been using my training partner to provoke a reaction from me.

Although I achieved most of my running success under the tutelage of Alan Scott, a coach from Hawick, it was John Dawson who got me started in spikes. To begin with I'd accompany established Kelso rugby players such as Andrew Ker, Bob Monaghan and

Bob Hogarth to his sprint classes and was more or less left to my own devices. But, after being convinced that I was serious about improving my speed and being blessed with a competitive nature, John began to concentrate more and more of his attentions on me. It was only because John had so many other irons in the fire that I switched coaches, for he was certainly a deep thinker about the sport – as my Mum learned to her cost in the local chemist's one day! John, a former New Year Sprint winner himself whose remarkable accomplishment in throwing Asian athletics into turmoil is chronicled in a previous chapter, believed in rubbing runners' legs down with methylated spirit. According to John, meths contained properties that toned the muscles, and so what if it made his runners stink to high heaven! That was nothing, anyway, to the stink in our household when my Mum, on her umpteenth visit to the chemist requesting this secret 'speed lotion', was quietly taken aside and asked, 'Are you sure your son is having the spirit rubbed on to his legs, Mrs Tait? It's most unusual to be dispensing so much of this spirit to the same person and, well, it's not unheard of for some people to drink meths as a cheap form of alcohol.' Now, I've been suspected of being many things in my time. But a meths drinker?

Rugby players have long turned to the track in the search for an extra yard of pace, and Scottish internationals of recent vintage such as Peter Dods and Greg Oliver both enjoyed some success. Keith Suddon of Hawick and Harry Hogg of Jed-Forest are others who have cashed in on their running abilities on the pro circuit. You have to commend for effort, too, a former Edinburgh second-row forward who had better remain nameless but who ventured down to Meadowbank athletics track one summer's evening to consult a sprint coach and was invited to demonstrate what passed for his technique. Clearly the coach had marked this student of his science down as a carthorse. 'Have you', he inquired as the big fellow pulled up alongside him, 'been to see a blacksmith?'

Every player can use the off-season to advantage, whether it is to gain extra pace, bulk up or, perhaps more importantly nowadays, recharge batteries. An alternative sport such as sprinting can provide an element of competition that will make training more fun and freshen the mind for the winter ahead, but off-season activity should always be balanced. Boxing, too, is a sport which offers advantages to rugby players. Hitting pads builds up a sense of rhythm and squaring up to an opponent with right or left foot forward between their legs simulates the in-face approach required for crash tackling. But sprinting is ideal for sharpness, and switching from boots to light-weight spikes can enable a player to gradually lengthen his running stride, which will pay huge dividends on the rugby field. But too much emphasis on sprint work will effectively burn the legs off a player and leave him feeling listless by halfway through the ensuing rugby season.

Energy is obtained through building up muscle tissue in the gym, which can create a real feeling of well-being. I recommend a rugby player do that first and then move outdoors into sprinting. Of course, players have plenty of time on tour to train with weights. But I am convinced that tours are on borrowed time in this new era, and that by staying home a player can enjoy freedom from the pressure that stems from being judged by results, yet still look to the future. There are new lifting techniques to be explored and different coaches that can be consulted. It was during the off-season, for example, that I was able to speak with Edgar Curtis, an American with a background in power lifting who had been brought in to assist the Leeds rugby league team. Edgar showed me lifting skills that quickly enhanced my muscle bulk, but the impact of his teachings would have been lessened had I been required to play at the same time.

In seeking the balance between power and pace, I often use the 'menagerie method' of summer training. For the first six weeks I think of myself as being in 'elephant training' – meaning that everything I do in the gym has to be of a heavyweight nature, and the pace is understandably slow. During this period the diet sheet goes out the window and I treat myself by eating more or less what I like. Then, in the weeks leading up to the new season, I put myself in antelope mode. The antelope is a lithe creature which lives on its wits and is swift across the ground. Everything is now geared to improving my speed and reactions, and I know I have topped up my strength levels so I have something to draw upon when concentrating on aerobic, as opposed to anaerobic, fitness.

There is so much that can be done in terms of self-improvement during the summer, and a break from playing should not be confused with a holiday, by any means. I know that Doddie Weir, for example, is bound to benefit in the long term from making himself unavailable for Scotland's 1998 trip to Fiji and Australia in order to undertake regular and sustained work in the Newcastle gymnasium. Doddie will emerge bigger, stronger and totally refreshed for the World Cup, and it is worth remembering that season 1999–2000 will end with a British Lions tour. That's another reason why Doddie – who has a lot to make up for after being invalided out of the last tour by an opponent's vicious kick to the knee – is right to lie low.

In the old days before rugby union went professional, tours contained a large element of rest and relaxation as well as the chance to work daily on fitness. When I first toured with Scotland, to North America in 1985, there was an educational and social element involving receptions laid on by Caledonian societies and local politicians. There were even sight-seeing trips. Amidst such a hectic whirl, how we managed to fit in our own cocktail parties at 6 p.m. most evenings I'll never know! It undoubtedly helped, though, that the opposition was mostly of a scratch nature, and did it really matter anyway if we defeated teams with names like the Grizzlies and the Wolverines whom nobody had heard of or could relate to? Nowadays the vast majority of players who go on tour are under the coach's gaze on a daily basis. Both parties are probably sick of the sight of each other come spring and need a break. Really the summer should be spent wishing and hoping for the season to come around again, not slogging it out from one destination to the next.

There was also a perceived need at one time to find out about players. How would they co-operate with colleagues? Would they fit into a general pattern of play? Would they prove disruptive? Coaches don't need access to that information when they have players under supervision all day. And only Tests are important in terms of determining a world pecking order, and what's the point in lining up preliminary opposition for tourists so as to boost their prospects for the one or possibly two matches that matter? That was all right in the days when the length of journey had to be justified, but not any more. Can you countenance, say, a top footballing country being offered the chance to play Hearts, Rangers and Celtic before going into the main event against Scotland at Hampden Park? I can't.

Nowadays the Super 12 provincial series has shown how easily teams can nip over to another continent for a game, with the effects of altitude reduced by playing shortly after arrival. Also, the need to go off the beaten track to undertake a bit of missionary work has been removed by television, especially with dedicated sports channels bringing the very best into so many living-rooms. That's not to say that tours of a developmental nature should not be held, though, as they can prove very useful, particularly those involving younger players, as can club safaris at the beginning of each season when minds are fresh and muscles keen.

Even then results should be secondary, and when I was at Widnes we'd undertake a week-long trip to Anglesey every pre-season. There we would do heavy training in the morning, and I'd make sure I paired up with team-mate Barry Dowds because he was superb on the weights. The afternoon would be set aside for outdoor activities such as canoeing, abseiling, horse-riding and golf. Evenings were spent in the bar building up team spirit to the extent that before our first game of the season, a Charity Shield clash with Wigan, we were visited in the dressing-room by Kevin Tamati, a good friend of our captain, Kurt Sorensen, who was due to undertake commentary duties. When Tamati left our company he went behind the microphone to predict that, having seen the condition of the Widnes team, our Wigan opponents didn't stand an earthly. He was right, too. We won because we were buzzing after the break and, believe me, we were no angels during that week at Anglesey. Rather Doug Laughton, our coach, got the balance between work and play in an unfamiliar environment absolutely spot on.

The main justification for touring is to fill the coffers of host unions, but if players continue to undertake overseas ventures in such a worn-out state that it reflects on their performance the exercise will soon be counter-productive. I took some flak for declaring myself unavailable for Scotland's tour of Australia and Fiji earlier this year along with the likes of Doddie, Gary Armstrong and Tony Stanger, but I make no apologies for doing so. I am trying to play a long game and not just be around come the next World Cup but be playing well into the bargain. By the time of the World Cup I'll be 35, but that need not preclude a contribution. By touring when I most definitely wasn't up for the challenge I'd have been cheating my own ambitions and, more importantly, the team. When Newcastle's domestic season eventually wound up with the Sanyo Challenge victory over a World

XV in what was my first ever appearance at Twickenham, there were just three days before the Scotland tour got under way in Fiji. The season would have felt like a treadmill. Because of rugby league's switch to summer and the Lions tour to South Africa, had I gone down under I wouldn't have had a summer without rugby for three years.

Even then, sensing Scotland's cupboard was rather bare – with all due respect to the younger members of the squad – I was prepared to strike a compromise whereby I would fly out just before the two Australian Tests. In the circumstances this didn't seem to me un-reasonable and I think Jim Telfer would have been agreeable. But there were rumblings from within the camp of preferential treatment, so I sat on my hands. I'm so glad I did. I'd just have been a liability. Mind you, if I had been asked to go along as a coach that might have been different, because it seems to me that our players are simply not used to defending against teams operating at pace. I've experienced that pace and managed to cope – largely due to groundwork done in rugby league where, significantly, major tours only come along every three or four years. There may be a negative side to the fact that rugby league isn't as internationally renowned as rugby union, but one of the benefits, for sure, is less need to drop in on global rivals every summer.

One other area where the close-season break can be vital is the chance to experiment with vitamin supplements. Here people are liable to throw their hands up in horror and immediately think: 'Drugs!' Believe me, that's not what I'm about to preach. It is many years since I first took Creatine – which, let me be clear, is a muscle-building substance but a legal alternative to anabolic steroids. I know there was a bad reaction to Creatine in the media recently when it was suspected of contributing to the deaths of three wrestlers in the United States. But it subsequently emerged that the wrestlers had dehydrated themselves by training on bicycles while wearing rubber suits. Others have suffered through taking well in excess of the recom-mended dosage, in one case the equivalent of 300 lbs of steak. This kind of irresponsible usage can lead to kidney damage, according to the British Olympic Association, but taking Creatine in moderation is a different matter altogether.

Creatine is a naturally produced substance which comes from the body but only in small quantities. Basically it speeds up time required to recover from training sessions. Creatine helps restore a substance in the muscle known as ATP which enables the muscle to go on contracting and replenishing itself much more quickly. Various forms of Creatine – pills, powder and even chewing-gum – are available, and I tend to sprinkle a teaspoonful a day on my breakfast cereal for six weeks at a time, usually pre-season. After that I tend to come off it because I don't think the body should become accustomed to it. It must also be acknowledged that the product is relatively new, which means a school of thought exists suggesting that it might be best to wait a while before coming to conclusions about its value. But I know of numerous rugby players, footballers and athletes at various levels who already take Creatine, and as the oval-ball game becomes more professional it is inevitable that every possible avenue to success will be explored.

I stress that Creatine is legal and recommend it as an acceptable aid in small doses. When I think, too, of how much damage is caused to sporting talent by alcohol misuse, any concern I might have about using a vitamin supplement to gain an edge diminishes considerably. Indeed some believe that Scotland, Wales and Ireland have long had a justifiable reputation for being nations of big drinkers. In the sporting revolution that is currently taking place, each of these countries is now getting its comeuppance.

On the other hand, sport should be given the resources to lead the quest for a fitter, healthier society, and I like to think I might have something to contribute towards achieving that goal.

CHAPTER TEN

A League of Nations?

By mid-1998 the enlightened amongst Scotland's rugby union administrators were willing to concede, privately at least, that Murrayfield's idea of creating two provincial teams as a vehicle for the professional game contained a fundamental flaw. The super-districts, as they are called, allowed players to train together full time. But lack of regular competitive fixtures outside a brief European Cup campaign was a huge drawback as far as I could see. Unless addressed quickly, this problem threatens to undermine the national team still further.

It may be that in Scottish rugby, market forces will ultimately determine that most, if not all, star players are based outside our shores and merely return from their full-time clubs for international duty, as happens with soccer in places like Ireland. Sugar-daddies in larger countries pay the salaries of players such as Roy Keane, who was unearthed in Eire and then sent to 'finishing school' in England. If something similar were to happen in rugby in Scotland, we could return to a meaningful domestic structure based on existing club sides paying what they can afford. That way, at least, the confusion which has been rife amongst supporters and which contributed to a massive decline in attendances as the weekly spotlight switched from club to provincial to international rugby and back again might finally be eliminated.

On the other hand, I believe that a preferred option – and one which would keep a nucleus of stars in Scotland as role models for youngsters, provide a focus of attention for the media and prove appealing for the fans – would be the creation of a British league. British leagues are long established in other sports such as speedway, athletics, basketball and ice hockey. And Cardiff City have played in the English Football League since 1920. So, as rugby union enters the twenty-first century, why not a British league in our sport as well?

There is just not the depth of playing resources – 10,630 senior participants at the latest count – to sustain a high-quality Scottish domestic competition. But clearly it is in the interests of all who have rugby union in these islands at heart that Scotland remain competitive, not least for the sake of the new Six Nations Championship due to involve Italy from the year 2000. For this reason I believe that many English club owners would react sympathetically if asked to incorporate Edinburgh–Borders and Glasgow–Caledonia in their set-up.

I believe that the lack of an intensive competition below international standard operating from week to week is the root cause of the Scottish team's decline to the extent that record defeats were suffered at the hands of France, South Africa and Australia in the 1997–98 season, not to mention first-time flops against Italy and Fiji. In making this assertion I go back to my career in rugby league, where there was always competition for club places to the extent that at Widnes I once found myself battling for the full-back slot alongside Jonathan Davies, Paul Atcheson and Stuart Spruce – each of us either a Great Britain last line or destined to become one.

At the moment it appears too easy for players to drop back into the comfort zone with – most damaging of all – international teams being selected on the basis of Scotland's last outing rather than on up-to-date club form. I would submit the Scottish Rugby Union are on the right lines with their super-districts, but the whole scheme will collapse unless doors open at a domestic level. And that must mean the Allied Dunbar English League, since I cannot see a truly meaningful European League in the near future. Rob Andrew, my old boss at Newcastle Falcons, is on record as saying he would be in favour of adding teams from Edinburgh and Glasgow, both of which are located in sizeable catchment areas. Northampton's Keith Barwell is another who is known to have been looking north with a view to spicing up English domestic competition.

Bear in mind, too, the following remarks I heard attributed to my old rugby league mentor, Doug Laughton: 'There's no room in sport now for a little smarty like me at a hick town like Widnes. The door is shut. It's the same in business. If you think you can open a successful corner shop or butcher's in the face of supermarkets, forget it. No hick town team is going to win Super League. Money will now play more of a part in shaping the format of our future sporting competitions and who wins them.'

I agree. Officials in Scotland must pull out all the stops and use their negotiating muscle to organise a British League, and if it comes to pass I hope they will look closely at the type of salary-capping scheme now operating successfully in Super League. The object of salary capping is, clearly, to prevent clubs from over-stretching themselves financially, and a by-product is a greater degree of competition compared with not long ago when Wigan dominated the sport. The fact that rank outsiders Sheffield Eagles could win this year's Challenge Cup was an incalculable boost, because the moment a sport becomes predictable it loses a vast amount of appeal.

Salary capping works on the principle of teams being permitted to spend no more than 50 per cent of their gross income on wages. Checks are made on a monthly basis and a sliding scale of fines has been rigidly applied. When Wigan were found to be allocating 70 per cent of their income to wages they were promptly fined £33,000 a month, which led to them offloading players, which, in turn, meant a fairer distribution of talent. The same sliding scale penalised teams who were up to 5 per cent over the limit with fines of up to £8,000 per month. I was surprised to learn too just how straightforward it has become to police the regulation by means of a central computer through which each club has to feed details of its income from all sources — gate receipts, sponsorships, corporate hospitality and so on. Maybe that is the way forward for rugby union in this country, although I have to admit it would be difficult for a governing body such as the Scottish Rugby Union to enter teams and be responsible for operating salary capping as well. No doubt an agreement could be reached, but that is for the future, when rugby union settles down after trying to cram into a couple of seasons the type of evolution that happened in rugby league over a century.

Of more immediate concern, as I see it, is the need to persuade owners of the lower-placed English clubs that they will not lose out through Scottish involvement. Increase the size of English competition if necessary, if it means a successful British League. Make no mistake, though, we would need the English on board, because they are at the heart of the commercial marketplace with prime appeal for sponsors and television. A Celtic Cup featuring the best of Ireland and Wales has been mooted but would carry nothing like the same clout as a competition involving Newcastle, Saracens, Bath and so on. Time is starting to run out if Scotland are to make an impression on the 1999 World Cup.

I believe we can still surprise a few people and have vowed to extend my career in the hope of playing in the global jamboree. With the World Cup now the yardstick by which countries are measured, I'd like to use this platform to suggest a few changes in the way the international team is run, based on my experience since becoming the first former rugby league player to return to the fold.

In rugby league it is inconceivable that players could stockpile caps the way they are able to do in rugby union without producing anything particularly out of the ordinary. Players just can't be on the top of their game for season upon season. Troughs are inevitable. But a glance at the Scottish selections of recent years suggests otherwise, even allowing for the importance of a degree of consistency and refusal to panic in the face of a bad result. The system has produced players who gladly coast between international matches, and one leading player, not without some justification, has acquired the nickname 'Tampax' because he spends one week in and three weeks out at club level.

I was particularly disturbed by the amount of internal disagreement which beset the Scotland team in 1997–98. It even extended to how the half-time interval should be spent. In the amateur era teams stayed on the pitch at the break but the advent of professionalism made it obligatory to return to the dressing-room, partly so that television could either recoup some of its financial outlay through advertising or update viewers with a results service from football, racing and so on. Celebrity summarisers also had to be given time to impart their views to the watching public. During last season a pattern emerged whereby Scotland teams fell away badly during the second half of matches. I had always thought of Scottish teams as being among the fittest and attributed the decline mainly to lack of concentration. An alternative theory was put forward by Craig Chalmers, however, who suggested the team should remain outdoors, attuning to the atmosphere. I had no sympathy with that view, especially when it was suggested that a few extra choruses of 'Flower of Scotland' might provide the inspiration needed. Either that or another helping of bagpipe music. You can overplay the emotional card, you know!

Half-time, for me, should be about relaxing and refuelling tired muscles, but others saw it differently. For example, David McLean, the Scottish team's fitness adviser, wanted us to be running about, while some players were heavily into stretching exercises. I put my tuppence worth in by declaring we should sit down, have a drink and generally unwind. Then, with the players relaxed, they might be more responsive to points made by the coaches. I've heard that the great Australian rugby league teams were never asked to take on board more than three points during the interval, because of the risk of confusing players who really needed to clear their heads and quickly recharge the batteries. Their coaches merely pointed out what could be improved and underlined what was going right. As often as not, players need reassurance during the break, not to be made to feel they have to take on board another barrage of tactical information.

Indeed, I have never forgotten a philosophy put around during the 1987 rugby union World Cup by Jim Blair, a Scot who was in charge of the All Blacks' physical conditioning and who has a proven track record in a number of other sports including yachting, where he has worked with America's Cup teams. Blair, now attached to Bath rugby union club, maintained that all the training sessions he supervised should be short, sharp and – as far as possible – simple. I still find it hard to accept the fact that Scotland's training sessions go on for so long. Maybe as professionalism settles down, the need for quality as opposed to quantity will be accepted. This, I suspect, applies equally to other walks of life, including business, where there is a culture which indicates that unless individuals are spending long hours at the workplace they can't be thinking about their job enough. The truly conscientious will know that problem-solving can some-times best be done by going outside the normal environment.

During the 1998 Five Nations Championship I became aware of occasions when those responsible for running the Scottish team were far too democratic in the way they opened up debates on matters that should have been resolved by delegation. For rugby union read the

Oxford Union. At least that's how it seemed to me at times, when team meetings that should have lasted a maximum of half an hour developed into debating chambers spanning up to three hours. One example of the Scottish squad's ability to turn a drama into a full-scale crisis concerned tactics for defending the blind side of a scrum. The only players really affected were the blind-side flanker, the No. 8, the scrum-half and the winger. Alas, everybody in the team got involved, and by the time we broke up and reconvened on the same issue I estimate a total of four and a half hours had been spent taking the system apart and putting it back together again. At the end of the day France still ran Scotland ragged down that channel, and I couldn't believe the way the debate had been allowed to drag on. I ended up urging Ian McGeechan to impose a system and tell the players to adhere to it, for that, to me, is the way coaches should work.

One of the problems with rugby union, especially where the Scottish team is concerned, is that nobody is accustomed to such responsibility and a lot of people spend a lot of time ensuring that any blame will be spread around. What should have happened was that the coach should have said, 'This is how you are doing it – and if it fails I cop the flak so you lot must consider your places in jeopardy, because next time I'll only be looking for players capable of carrying out my instructions properly.'

I think that sort of accountability will come eventually, with selectors destined to be a diminishing breed, as in football. Unfortunately that will be too late for Richie Dixon and David Johnston, the Scottish coaches removed from office immediately after the opening international of 1998, away to Italy, brought an extremely avoidable 25–21 defeat despite a winning platform having been established. Alas, we lacked the conviction to finish Italy off from 21–12 ahead, and I suspect it was partly through fear of losing. Time and again the consequences of defeat had been drummed into us. But you know what happens when you set an alarm clock and make a mental note that it is absolutely imperative you do not sleep in. The inevitable happens and you do. It was like that in Treviso.

Richie Dixon seemed to be in an extremely difficult situation, working under a director of rugby with the coaching pedigree of Jim Telfer, especially after the success of the Lions. I know that Jim tried very hard to give Richie space and I know how deeply upset he was when he was delegated to be the one to hand over the black spot. But Jim was always in the background, and one incident which summed up the situation occurred just prior to Richie's last match in charge.

Whenever I had watched videos of Scotland during the 1996–97 season I had been aware that players would take the ball into the tackle from where it was liable to go anywhere on impact. Scottish players were very weak in this department and nobody was really pulling them up on it. Watching the 1997 Italy match on video along with the squad, I made that very point about the ball being surrendered too easily. Afterwards, as I was walking out of the room, Jim Telfer pulled me to one side. I instantly thought I was going to get a rollocking for speaking my mind, judging by the way he grabbed me by the shoulder. However, he waited until everybody had left the room, then told me, 'Glad you pointed that out. It should have been said a long time ago.' I think Jim shared my frustration that the coaches were not preaching ball retention hard enough. Jim wanted that aspect to be emphasised, but at that stage he was in the background and not the front-line coach. So, how could he get the message across without treading too heavily on Richie's toes? I had come to his rescue. I could see that he was eager for a greater say, and when he was installed as caretaker coach after the Italy game I'm sure he was happy to be hands-on again. It was agreeable also to note David Leslie being groomed to take over when Telfer decides to call it a day, because he is a no-nonsense type who'll command plenty of respect.

It really was strange, after the success of the British Lions under their tutelage, to see Jim Telfer and Ian McGeechan in the wings, although I'm increasingly unsure about the latter's appointment as a consultant to Scotland. On the day Scotland played Wales at Wembley, Geech had to be with his club, Northampton, and the haste with which he was brought back into the national set-up did smack a bit of desperation to keep him out of England's clutches. And I hope Jim Telfer, outwardly philosophical about Scotland's summer defeat by Fiji, isn't starting to mellow too much.

But there was a time when Jim's intensive approach was in danger of being damaging. I heard through Gary Armstrong that some of the lads were pleased when I returned to the scene from league because I managed to lift some tension through being prepared to indulge in give-and-take. During my spell away it seemed I had developed a confidence some of them were lacking. When I was previously in rugby union the likes of Jim Renwick would crack jokes non-stop, with Keith Robertson, John Rutherford and Roy Laidlaw also capable of pulling legs during training sessions. Everything seemed to be ultra-serious when I went back, which is never conducive to getting the best out of people.

As I've said previously, I really rated David Johnston as a running back who, during the late '70s and early '80s, managed to ghost through gaps with grace and poise. But I found many of his ideas concerning defence difficult to accept on my return, and most were still in place when France arrived at Murrayfield in 1998 to pour through holes at an alarming rate. There had been no time between David's departure and the arrival of Roy Laidlaw with Ian McGeechan as consultant to really strip down the components of our defence and put things back together again.

David was a lightweight player in physical terms and he seemed more preoccupied with switches, loop passes and backs being launched at the opposition from a variety of angles. The emphasis at times seemed to be more on making pretty patterns with criss-cross runs and floated passes than running on to the ball at real pace and hitting hard. Backs have also got to be looking at ways of ensuring the opposition ball isn't posted back, which often means wrestling the carrier to the ground and turning him so that his body is between ball and support runners. By gearing the approach to gifted runners, we didn't seem to have a solid base to work off. Aggression was never part of David's make-up as a player and so it was unlikely he would coach it. He was a footballer. But the trick is to find footballers with physical presence.

Having said all that, I know that David was a big fan of the powerhouse Stirling centre Ian Jardine when he was fit. And to further acknowledge that his style can work in certain circumstances, the French have shown plenty of flair, particularly through Thomas Castaignède, star of the 1998 Five Nations series despite standing only 5ft 9ins tall and weighing in at under 12st 11lbs when dripping wet. But to reach the top in rugby requires a mean streak as well, and I sometimes wondered if David Johnston was too nice. It was certainly hard for me going back to rugby union where drift defence is a big ploy. I prefer a system where you go up on an attacker who is gradually pushed out.

On the way to capturing the Allied Dunbar Premiership with Newcastle, Inga Tuigamala and I had very few tries scored against us. Everybody said we defended in the three-quarters as a flat four, which meant taking the wingers up and leaving Rob Andrew to look after the stand-off if he came through on the break. As far as Inga and I were concerned, we concentrated purely on taking anybody who came through the middle. It might have looked a dumb way to defend but it takes a lot to unlock that system, because even if the winger gets the ball it is one on one with his marker, leaving the full-back to cover in behind. Letting somebody through the middle is almost impossible for the full-back to defend, so I have always argued that if the defence is breached, let it be on the outside, and hopefully the full-back is good enough to cover. If you are always drifting away from attackers, it is inevitable that they are going to take the holes that are left behind.

Drift defence, in my opinion, is old-fashioned. I'd rather have a race across the field so that the winger ends up with the ball in his hands and five defenders around him. I'd advise all aspiring centres to go up and attack the ball. And, until the ball has left the opponent's hands, I can't see the point in a drift defence. Readjusting to defensive alignments was the hardest part of my return from rugby league, and there's no denying that Gregor Townsend and I were caught out a few times in our centre pairing. Gregor is obviously used to drift defence. He has been groomed in that style. On the other hand, I was used to going straight up, man on man. But we got our differences sorted out in the end. Against France in 1998, though, I felt that Gregor was setting off for the incoming full-back before the centre had even passed the ball to him. Consequently we left 'open doors' through which the opposition were happy to stroll.

The biggest victim in all of this was Kenny Logan, who was used to a different system at his club, Wasps. I knew he was concerned about it. Basically, with Gregor chosen at outside centre he had the type of influence I wanted on the defence. I certainly like wingers, if a full-back comes up out wide, to hit the full-back and let the centres cover in behind to claim the wingers. Gregor, on the other hand, was adamant that he wanted Kenny to stay out wide and he would cover the full-back's intrusion. Poor Kenny didn't know if he was coming up or going wide, and he lost his international place as a consequence.

One match earlier we had gutsed out a win over a fairly ordinary Irish side, while against Wales we kept their centres, Scott Gibbs and Allan Bateman, pretty quiet, and that was down to asking more questions of the attack. Whenever the southern hemisphere teams visit, they teach us something new and it is back to the drawing-board again. No sooner have we mastered it than they have moved on again. To combat them teams must meet force with force. That's how the Lions turned up trumps. We went straight up in the Springboks' faces.

My message, really, is that players have to be sure in their own minds how they want to play in defence and get it all sorted out in advance. There was a lot of misunderstanding in that French game that cost us dearly, and I lay in my bed that night – I take defeats very personally – trying in vain to put my finger on where Scotland were going wrong. It was when I focused on the defensive systems that things fell into place and I began to explain our shortcomings to myself.

Making substitutions is another aspect of rugby league that has been around for some time, yet rugby union seemed to struggle to come to terms with its arrival, particularly in the Dixon–Johnston era at Murrayfield. On one occasion during the 1997–98 season a front-row change was made against Australia with Scotland backed up on their own line, while the length of time taken to get Duncan Hodge on the pitch against South Africa when Tony Stanger retired hurt contributed to the visitors having space in which to engineer a vital try which set them on the way to an impressive victory.

In rugby league, one of my roles was to 'spy' for Doug Laughton at Widnes and let him know which of my team-mates were tiring. There was nothing sneaky about the task. It was expected of a senior player to send back signals. Doug would then keep a closer watch on the individuals concerned and decide whether or not to take them off.

Jim Telfer had more grasp of the extra dimension offered by substitutions on account of his work with the British Lions, when he had 13 matches calling the shots from the sidelines. Jim, like any other coach running a bench, needed information to be relayed from the field and I took responsibility for telling him at Wembley when we played Wales that Damian Cronin was starting to get tired, and I didn't see anything wrong with that. There was no shame as far as Damian was concerned. Obviously he wants to think of himself as an 80-minute man, but older players in his position at the heart of the forward grind have got to be used sensibly.

I'm a great believer in the 'fresh legs' theory, and the notion that being subbed is somehow demeaning has to be changed so that players don't take it as a reflection on how they have been playing. Fresh legs can add a lot to a team. At Leeds we had three props, Neil Harman, Harvey Howard and Esene Faimalo, who rotated, and they had the system working perfectly. It is an area where coaches can speak to players and say 'Give us 60 minutes of your best rugby'. Given such guidelines a player can go out and fully express himself, rather than ask himself if he will last the pace.

Scotland have also got themselves into the habit of holding debriefings on the morning after a match, and I am not 100 per cent behind this idea. The day, or rather the early morning, after a game is when I think players should be trying to switch off a bit, not be dragged into a room in a hotel to learn what they have done wrong – or got right! A debriefing is something you can leave and digest and maybe come to terms with a couple of days later, although I realise that this is always easier to put into effect at club level than with an international squad liable to disperse in many different directions.

In rugby league we used to have a players' meeting a couple of days after a game where the accent was firmly on honest appraisal. Players were actually encouraged to be forthright in saying things about the guys they were alongside in 'the trenches'. Criticism was never meant in a hurtful way. Rather these sessions were intended to provide a forum in which points that needed to be made could be made. Players and coaches could say what they felt had to be said without grudges being held against them. Anything raised in that debriefing room remained confidential and it was agreed that nobody would take any comment home to his wife or into the public domain. There was a common bond of secrecy, and in that environment a lot of necessary truths came out. If you were not happy with the way a colleague was playing you told him and tried to sort it out – there and then. That, to me, was better than going to the pub and saying to somebody after six pints that you thought he was playing poorly.

For a player, criticism is essential. It's out there and has to be accepted and acted upon wisely and positively. I've been criticised many times, and while I don't like being told certain things, I go away, digest the information and come back stronger for it in trying to change, if I believe that is necessary. At the same time, some criticism from ex-internationals is starting to get out of order. I feel that Stuart Barnes and Mike Stephenson, the Sky Television duo fronting union and league coverage respectively, are particularly hard-hitting, often for the sake of it. Former Scotland captains David Sole and Gavin Hastings have also gone to extremes in the way they take their successors apart. Didn't they ever miss a tackle or drop a pass? In Gav's case he missed a few really soft ones, while Soley criticised Kenny Logan and Gregor Townsend for smiling at the final whistle after the French international this year. For pity's sake.

Once a game that brings defeat is over, everybody in the team, I'm sure, is sickened by the result. But there are times when you have to put on a bit of a face. Players can smile at the opposition and shrug their shoulders as if to say, 'Ah well, it was your day, but we'll get you next time.' Or they can smile because they know a member of the opposition well enough to have become friendly, perhaps from touring together with the Lions or the Barbarians. At the end of the day you can either put on a front or you can charge off to the changing-room. I've seen guys do both.

For example, Martin Offiah ran from the field following Great Britain's World Cup final defeat in 1992 and wouldn't go up the famous Wembley staircase for his runner-up medal. Martin was slated in the media for his actions and got all sorts of abuse, including comments to the effect that he failed to act responsibly and show youngsters how to deal with defeat. Sometimes you are left in a lose-lose situation, because only the player really knows how he feels.

I couldn't have had too much criticism on the pitch in 1998 with Scotland, though, because I ended up being voted Famous Grouse Scottish Player of the Five Nations. It was especially satisfying to claim the award having finished runner-up the previous season (to Doddie Weir) when I had entered the action halfway through. Getting amongst the tries never does any harm, and at one stage I was bidding to become the first Scot since the 1930s to score in four successive Five Nations Championship games after crossing the try-line in Ireland to add to my haul of three from two appearances at the end of the '97 campaign. It meant a lot to finish ahead of – in descending order – Gary Armstrong, Adam Roxburgh, Craig Chalmers and Rob Wainwright in that poll, and I was surprised at how quickly news of my success spread among friends and team-mates at Newcastle. Also, thinking back to my rugby league career, I seemed to make a habit of being runner-up to the likes of Ellery Hanley at Leeds and either Jonathan Davies or Martin Offiah at Widnes. It was maybe just as well, too, that I had a substantial lead going into the final match, against England, which was, I felt, my worst display since returning to Scottish blue. The reason can be summed up in two words: Phil Larder.

A former rugby league coach, Larder was brought in by England to organise their defence, and it was clear to me that in the Calcutta Cup match I had been picked out along with Gregor Townsend for tighter than usual marking. Throughout the afternoon I was frus-tratingly aware of getting man and ball almost simultaneously, with the consequence that when we tried to run passes we were hurried, leading to turnovers. To all intents and purposes Larder confirmed to me afterwards that England had tried to close down Gregor and myself – which was, I suppose, a compliment. The sort of planning Phil was required to undertake is something that appeals to me.

If the day ever dawns when I am put in charge of a Scotland team, I wouldn't have any problem with selecting players who have grown up learning their rugby overseas, provided they were eligible through family or residency. There was some disquiet over the decision by Scotland in 1998 to include on the bench against England the Northampton flanker Budge Pountney, who is from the Channel Islands but whose grandmother hails from Scotland. Under inter-national rules that made Pountney eligible for Scotland and I would have had no qualms about calling him up, although others were quite voluble in their opposition.

Discontent at selection procedures surfaced again when Scotland prepared to fly out on tour to Fiji with Gordon Simpson, a New Zealander of Scottish extraction, and Matthew Proudfoot, a giant South African prop whose ancestors hailed from Dumfriesshire, in the 35-strong party. The fact that both had been in the country only a matter of weeks before being called up irritated some. But if they were good enough and eligible by birthright, they had to be chosen, in my book. The same went for Glenn Metcalfe, Cameron Mather and Shaun Longstaff, all New Zealand born but qualified by residency to wear the thistle, while it spoke volumes for the commitment of Newcastle second row Richard Metcalfe that he should have hired a genealogist to prove his Scottish connection.

Such an attitude may sound rich coming from somebody who went to great lengths to ensure his children, Michael and Zoey, were born in Scotland at a time when he was based in the north of England. But when it comes to international rugby, there is more to be gained overall by creating a winning team than standing on a moral principle. Give the public a few victories and they won't worry where the Scotland XV is drawn from. You'd better believe it.

One other area which has concerned me is the man-management of some Scottish teams in recent years. By this stage in a sportsman's reminiscences it is customary to have put oneself in selectors' shoes and listed a so-called 'dream team' based on the best of old rivals. I have already gone beyond the realms of the fantasy XV. I decided Cammy Glasgow would be capped for Scotland against France at Parc des Princes in 1997.

I was just one match back into my international rugby union career with Scotland when a reminder occurred of just how far some officials have to go before they can be considered worthy man-managers in the professional game. There were times before the barriers came down when I experienced frustration at not knowing whether I'd ever be welcomed back to play out the final years of my career amongst friends at grass-roots level. Such frustrations were born out of wanting more than I was fairly entitled to expect from rugby, and they certainly paled into insignificance compared with the plight of Cammy Glasgow, a useful utility back from the Heriot's FP club, who had been on the fringes of the Scotland team for eight years.

Cammy was one of those guys who struck me as never having yearned to make a penny from his rugby skills. All he sought was a coveted cap, and for almost a decade it had been dangled in front of him – before being whipped away cruelly on one occasion just as he thought the golden moment had arrived. To say that Cammy was treated shabbily would be something of an understatement, and I'm quietly proud of how I used my position within the team to engineer a reliable servant's arrival on the international scene.

First called on to the bench against Fiji in 1989, Cammy was ordered to warm up pitch-side in preparation for going on to gain a cap before an injury scare subsided. Fair enough. In those days rugby union had not introduced tactical substitutions and the cap chance disappeared for a while. But the authorities really blundered with Cammy immediately prior to the 1995 World Cup in South Africa when Gavin Hastings retired in the closing moments of the final warm-up game, a 49–16 win over Romania at Murrayfield. Instead of elevating Cammy to ensure that every member of the 30-strong squad travelled as a fully fledged international, the powers that be decided to send Scott Hastings out into the dying embers of a match well and truly won. Tactically that might have been in keeping with pre-ordained plans, but with two minutes remaining and Scotland coasting it made no sense whatsoever. Had they taken the obvious step, the entire squad would have gained a boost at one player's obvious delight and there would have been a uniformity about the travelling party. As it was they risked an element of disillusionment which could have festered.

Even then the management had a chance to redeem the situation, with Scotland drawn to face the Ivory Coast in their opening match of the tournament. Had they played with their legs tied together the Scots could have been relied upon to cruise home against the shock African qualifiers. But a perceived need to put as many points on the board as possible in case scoring differential became a factor in qualification – the eventual result was 89–0 – militated against Cammy's chances of gaining a cap.

When we headed across the channel for the final Five Nations international to be played at the Parc des Princes before France moved to the new St Denis Stadium, I was made aware of Cammy's close calls and resolved to manipulate the situation in his favour. There was nothing really at stake for Scotland other than trying to perform creditably, although I'm pleased to relate I became only the fifth Scot to score a couple of tries in an away match against the French.

All week Cammy had chattered on about how desperate he was to get that elusive cap, and since he'd passed his 30th birthday it was reasonable to assume that the concluding international of the season might represent his only remaining opportunity. When I mentioned that I'd try to accommodate him by coming off towards the end if he still hadn't been capped, his face lit up. I, for my part, saw little harm in such an arrangement, depending, of course, on how a match Scotland went on to lose 47–20 was unfolding. 'Will you come off for me? Will you really come off and let me get a cap?' pleaded Cammy with a voice betraying schoolboy-type anticipation. Clearly it meant so much to him to follow in the footsteps of his father, Ronnie, a prominent international in the 1960s. I could easily identify with that, given that my own father had shone a beacon for me to follow.

It had been common practice for years in rugby league to quietly withdraw and allow a colleague on to the pitch, mainly so that he could share in bonus schemes – and on that score, incidentally, I found it strange that Scotland players were to receive £2,500 for the Paris match – win, lose or draw – with substitutes guaranteed a minimum of £1,500. On other occasions in league we would be aware of a colleague needing to be capped in order to fulfil another clause in his contract which offered additional payment for representative recognition. So it wasn't uncommon to say to a player, 'Here, give me a break if the result is settled, and I'll return the favour if I can one day.'

During the course of the Paris international I actually got whacked on the shin, and with Newcastle playing Rugby in a Division Two match the following day, discretion was very much the better part of valour as far as I was concerned. I have to confess also that the arrangement I had with Newcastle at that time was on a no-play, no-pay basis, so I was thinking about lost wages if I aggravated any damage and failed to report for club duty.

I informed Martin Rennison, the Scotland physio, that I was toiling, but he wasn't keen on the idea of taking me off. With the battle well and truly lost I called Martin over a second time, but he informed me that there were only seven minutes remaining and that I should try to stick it out. Obviously Martin had his orders – and I couldn't help thinking that they were based on saving the £1,000 due if a sub came off the bench.

In the end I took the decision for myself, saying I was coming off and that any tight-fisted official could like it or lump it. As I made my way to the side of the pitch I saw Cammy running past, and the thrilled expression on his face is something I treasure. I should have reacted a lot quicker to protect my injury and Cammy ought to have had more than the last few minutes. But never mind. He got his reward and my conscience was clear as far as cheating the authorities was concerned, because I was too crocked to turn out for Newcastle against Rugby.

Of course, I could see the SRU's point of view about not wanting to devalue caps won by previous generations when they could now be granted relatively easily. But the game was in the middle of an epoch-breaking phase, and by creating another international the SRU had, unwittingly, produced someone with that little bit of extra kudos who can now fly the flag for rugby with greater credibility – even on account of just a few minutes on the pitch. Well worth the extra £1,000 in terms of public relations. If only the bosses had thought that way.

To me, Cammy's situation had much wider implications and summed up a lack of realisation on the part of the authorities that rugby in the professional era has to sell itself harder. Doors will always open and invitations will drop through the letter-box for Cammy Glasgow, Scotland international. On the other hand, Cammy Glasgow, nearly man, won't turn too many heads. Significantly, in the final minutes of that Paris match the French sent all their substitutes out so that each player could say he had taken part in a Grand Slam-clinching victory. Twenty-one players going around France sharing their experience as opposed to fifteen makes better commercial sense, as I'm sure you'll agree.

Once again, though, our rivals had been seen to be proactive, with Scotland merely reacting to change – just as we had done at the 1987 World Cup when the squad returned with uncapped players despite predictable victories against Zimbabwe and Romania. Gary Callander and Jerry Richardson were a couple of players who went out there just to make up the numbers. Meanwhile, players who could have done with a rest before facing the All Blacks in the quarter-finals were obliged to soldier on.

Until we get matters right off the field it is hardly fair to expect international fortunes to improve on it – but, of course, the trans-formation to professionalism was never going to be easy. It was just a pity the authorities had spent so much time putting it off. It was ironic, too, that when professionalism did arrive, rugby league, the sport they had tried so hard to keep at arm's length, should have been the code to suffer. I've often wondered whether rugby union officials would have looked down their noses at rugby league quite so much if they had known earlier what they know now. Also, would they have rushed so often for the moral high ground from where they would preach the virtues of amateurism?

If I were called into Murrayfield next week, though, and handed a development role, my first lesson would be that Scotland need to develop the southern hemisphere mentality we see in the Super 12 competition, especially now that England have done so – with due allowance being made for that farcical 76–0 defeat by Australia in a match tagged on to the front of their New Zealand tour when so many stalwarts were missing, recuperating from a hard domestic campaign. England could well reap the benefits in 1999 of their stars staying at home.

I suspect, too, that the possibility of attracting investors to Scottish rugby is brighter than many current officials are prepared to admit. Scotland has always had a proud rugby tradition and the country stands on the brink of an economic revolution with the advent of a parliament in Edinburgh. Who says the wealth is always to be concentrated in the south-east of England? I remember watching a television documentary recently which claimed that Canada has the highest standard of living in the world despite living next door to the United States.

It could be the same with us.

CHAPTER ELEVEN

So, Where Now?

I am becoming increasingly convinced that a common code of rugby could be just around the corner. Although rugby union and rugby league will still exist in pretty much their present forms, the growing influence of television may ensure that a hybrid version of the oval-ball game will spring up early in the new millennium.

There are too many diehards around for both the existing codes to disappear altogether. And rightly so. But such is the power of television, requiring something of broad appeal to slot in between advertisements, a compromise might be reached and a sport to be called, say, mega rugby will be born.

I am in no doubt that 'mega rugby' will have much going for it as a free-flowing, handling sport with that vital element of physical contact calculated to make audiences wince and feel glad they're not on the receiving end of the tackle. Mega rugby will never overtake football in popularity terms, of course. But especially by ensuring a wholesome family image and providing matches devoid of any crowd disturbances, it will fulfil a role worldwide that American football so desperately craves. Gridiron has tried hard to fit the bill but an insistence on too much protective clothing for its participants and complex rules has been a turn-off to many outside the traditional heartland.

Mega rugby will attract a global audience and be based more on rugby union than on rugby league, but it will feature top players from both codes. There is a school of thought that says if what became rugby league hadn't broken away from rugby union in acrimonious fashion back in 1895, the latter would be a very different game today. The perceived logic of those who support the theory is that rugby union administrators knew all those years ago that they would have to create a more spectator-friendly game by means of law changes – but they were always beaten to the punch by their rivals. Consequently it was beneath the dignity of rugby union to be seen to be borrowing any variations from a code they quickly came to despise for having the effrontery to defy their authority on the subject of broken-time payments to players requiring leave of absence from work for matches. Everyone has their price, though, and money is already helping to create something akin to what those early rugby union administrators probably had in mind, although it is difficult to countenance them scrapping lineouts the way league did in 1897.

Moves towards that hybrid code are already under way in the southern hemisphere, where, it would appear, the Super 12 series embracing the best of provincial rugby union in South Africa, New Zealand and Australia has been founded upon a set of law inter-pretations conducive to a running and handling extravaganza but – significantly – also featuring big hits and collisions. It was very much apparent to the Lions in South Africa during 1997 that we too were playing Super 12 rules, with referees telling players not to touch the ball in rucks. You know you are wasting your time, anyway, by burrowing if the opposition have possession secured, and fortunately we had a few games in which to adapt before arriving at the Test series.

Apart from the fact that it is much less predictable than league, and a degree more sophisticated, basically what makes Super 12 so appealing is the fact that the ball is rarely contested on the ground. Consequently those static pile-ups which can squeeze the life out of any rugby spectacle are reduced. In fact, television viewers can usually hear Super 12 referees calling out 'blue ball' or 'red ball', meaning the side not in possession has to leave well alone and desist from trying to spoil.

I've always believed that rugby of either code is the most thrilling of pastimes when played to win; it is something less endearing when the object is to avoid losing. The trick, in a professional sport, is to find the balance that recognises both the fact that players will try to wrest an advantage by almost any means and a sense of obligation to those who make the whole exercise possible – the spectators. With quick, clean possession from rucks, backs have a better chance of exhibiting the skills that spectators obviously want to see. The downside is that there is not the vigorous rucking which the blood-thirsty may particularly enjoy! The ruck has been described by no less an authority than Allan Hosie, the former international rugby union referee and now a dedicated administrator, as the engine on which the 15-a-side code runs. Allan's right. Remove the ruck and there is no vehicle for keeping play continuous at breakdown situations. It is a feature as distinct as the play-the-ball in league.

The play-the-ball scenario, however, affords defences vital moments in which to regroup, and the essence of union is its flow outside the set-pieces and the opportunities to test defences as they rapidly try to regroup. With fewer players required to commit them-selves to rucks and strung out across the pitch at breakdowns, the resemblance between Super 12 and league is at its most apparent – except that there remains room for 15 players to indulge in vital covering chores and too often in league, it must be acknowledged, a try is scored once the first line of cover is broken.

Super 12 has taken the basic handling skills of league and woven them into a set of rules which still gives defences a sporting chance of exerting some authority, and that's important. It wouldn't do for rugby to become like basketball, where the team in possession invariably holds on to the ball until a scoring chance is created. Sure, there is criticism at times that matches are just too free-scoring. But as long as the opportunity exists for players to turn over possession through their strength and technique in the tackle, too much predictability can be avoided. Occasionally I have heard Super 12 described as 'rugby league with lineouts', and there is a theory that if teams have not found their way past the fringe defence with an initial series of drives, they will resort to kicking for position in a not dissimilar fashion to rugby league as the sixth tackle beckons.

Scrums will certainly be needed in the new cross-code game, because without them the pace of play would be overwhelming. As things stand it is little wonder that southern hemisphere teams already seem to have a bit extra on opponents over here. When the ball is alive for such long periods, players are able to boost their lung capacities through all the chasing around.

As I said earlier, television will be the catalyst for change, especially with pay-per-view schemes on the horizon offering a dramatic increase in the amount of live sport that can be beamed into homes. Both rugby league and rugby union have already enjoyed massive infusions of cash from the Rupert Murdoch Corporation. At some point the paymaster might suggest he can live without writing two cheques when one will suffice and ask, 'How much will it cost to get the pair of you together, boys?'

In 1996 the unthinkable for many people happened when Bath rugby union club met Wigan rugby league club in two matches, each attempting to master the other's code. The next step may well be a third encounter featuring well-known names playing under a compromise set of laws. As to the likely timescale, Super League's £87.5 million deal with Murdoch is due to expire at the end of the century. Could that signal the start of the marriage of the codes?

For sure, I was intrigued by an article earlier this year in the *Mail on Sunday* newspaper which suggested that plans were in the pipeline for a single code based on existing heartlands of union and league. The scheme was referred to as a life-boat package for top rugby league outfits if the Murdoch money wasn't renewed and the likes of Wigan and Leeds would be involved, it was claimed. I doubt whether such an occurrence will happen so close to home, but you never know, and a possible stepping-stone could be the emergence of rugby clubs boasting both union and league sections under the same umbrella organisation. That way bar revenue is maintained all year round and – dare I say it – all youngsters are introduced by means of the more simple league version.

Don't write off either the Scottish Rugby Union's ability to adjust to any change on that scale, having as far back as 1994 staged a match in Glasgow using experimental laws. That match was the brainchild of Allan Hosie and involved teams of 13-a-side. The general consensus, though, was that removing flankers created too much space for runners, with the result that defences were easily shredded.

Something they have done in Super 12 is retain a place for the 6ft 8ins giant alongside the will-o'-the-wisp scrum-half, and that ability to cater for all shapes and sizes is a part of rugby that is particularly appealing.

It would suit me to be coaching Super 12-type rugby in the near future and I believe the game in these shores is already moving in the right direction, although stronger refereeing, particularly in cracking down on players slowing up possession, would help. Statistics relating to the 1998 Five Nations Championship showed that the ball was, on average, in play for 31 minutes and 15 seconds of each match. Or 36 per cent of the time. Contrast that with two years previously, when the ball had been in play for an average of 26 minutes and 57 seconds, or 32 per cent of the game. Most revealing of all for me, though, is the fact that my Dad, who is an out-and-out rugby league aficionado, admits to being hooked on Super 12, which must mean that it bears more than a passing resemblance to what is served up at Workington, Widnes and Wigan.

Whatever unfolds for rugby at large, it is my ambition to be involved in coaching or fitness training at some point in the near future, and with that in mind I began some time ago compiling a video library of routines and drills which will surely come in useful.

There's a lot of water to flow under the bridge before the 1999 World Cup, but the aim is to reach that milestone and then reflect on the words of my former sprint coach John Dawson, who once told me, 'Anybody who is blessed with a talent never loses it. You maybe just stop doing whatever it was you are good at. But you never lose it.' I'll just stop doing it – and hopefully move on.

I couldn't have forgiven myself if I hadn't clambered down off the roof in the days when I was working as a slater to see how far my abilities in rugby would take me. And I knew that in order to maximise my potential I had to turn professional – something rugby union could not offer me in those days.

Soon it will be time to see how much of what I have learned can, in turn, be imparted to others, and I hope above all else that if I'm ever to be judged as a player it won't be on my final few years back in rugby union. Gavin Hastings, for one, remarked during the British Lions tour of South Africa that he had underestimated my ability to perform. The truth, as I saw it, was that Gavin was comparing me then with how I had played before going off to rugby league. I hope that any assessors remember that my peak years were in rugby league, on the way to becoming an oval-ball all-rounder who saw a bit of the world, lifted the occasional trophy, had a few laughs, met some great people . . . and got paid for it. What more could any sportsman ask?

Alan Tait's Career Record

Kelso Rugby Union Club

1982–83 – 13 appearances (7 tries)
1983–84 – 28 appearances (13 tries)
1984–85 – 21 appearances (12 tries)
1985–86 – 23 appearances (9 tries)
1986–87 – 22 appearances (14 tries)
1987–88 – 18 appearances (16 tries, 1 conversion and 2 drop goals)

Total appearances – 125
Total tries – 71

Widnes Rugby League Club

1987–88 – 3 appearances, all as substitute (1 try)
1988–89 – 39 appearances (16 tries and 1 drop goal)
1989–90 – 36 appearances (17 tries, 1 conversion and 2 drop goals)
1990–91 – 28 appearances (12 tries)
1991–92 – 30 appearances, including 1 as substitute (9 tries)

Total appearances – 136
Total tries – 55

Leeds Rugby League Club

1992–93 – 32 appearances (9 tries)
1993–94 – 34 appearances (11 tries)
1994–95 – 37 appearances (13 tries)
1995–96 – 16 appearances, including 3 as substitute (9 tries)
1996–97 – 7 appearances, including 3 as substitute (2 tries)

Total appearances – 126
Total tries – 44

Newcastle Rugby Union Club

1996–97 – 11 appearances (6 tries)
1997–98 – 29 appearances, including 1 as substitute (9 tries)

REPRESENTATIVE CAREER

Rugby League

1988–89
Great Britain v. France (2 Tests) – 1 try

1989–90
Great Britain v. New Zealand (2) – 2 tries
Great Britain v. France (2) – 1 try
Great Britain v. Papua New Guinea (2)

1991–92
Great Britain v. France

1992–93
Great Britain v. Australia – (World Cup final, substitute)
Great Britain v. France – 2 tries

1993–94
Great Britain v. New Zealand (3, all as substitute)

1994–95
Scotland v. Russia (Emerging Nations World Cup)
Scotland v. USA (Emerging Nations World Cup)
Scotland v. Cook Islands (Emerging Nations World Cup)

1995–96
Scotland v. Ireland – 1 try

Rugby Union

Scotland B

1984–85
Scotland B v. Ireland B
Scotland B v. France B

1985–86
Scotland B v. Italy
Scotland B v. France

1986–87
Scotland B v. Italy
Scotland B v. France

Scotland

1986–87
Scotland v. France (World Cup)
Scotland v. Zimbabwe (World Cup) – 2 tries
Scotland v. Romania (World Cup) – 2 tries
Scotland v. New Zealand (World Cup)

1987–88
Scotland v. Ireland
Scotland v. France
Scotland v. Wales
Scotland v. England

1996–97
Scotland v. Ireland – 1 try
Scotland v. France – 2 tries

1997–98
Scotland v. Australia
Scotland v. Italy – 1 try
Scotland v. Ireland – 1 try
Scotland v. France
Scotland v. Wales
Scotland v. England

British Lions

1997
Great Britain v. South Africa (2) – 1 try

RUGBY LEAGUE CLUB HONOURS

World Clubs' Challenge won with Widnes – 1989–90 (v. Canberra Raiders)
Club Championship won with Widnes – 1988–89
Challenge Cup runner-up with Leeds – 1993–94 and 1994–95 (v. Wigan)
Premiership won with Widnes – 1987–88 (v. St Helens), 1988–89 (v. Hull), 1989–90 (v. Bradford Northern)
Premiership runner-up with Widnes – 1990–91 (v. Hull)
Premiership runner-up with Leeds – 1994–95 (v. Wigan)
Regal Trophy won with Widnes – 1991–92 (v. Leeds)
Regal Trophy runner-up with Widnes – 1988–89 (v. Wigan)
Lancashire Cup won with Widnes – 1988–89 (v. Salford)

Charity Shield won with Widnes – 1988–89 (v. Wigan), 1989–90 (v. Wigan), 1990–91 (v. Wigan)
Charity Shield runner-up with Leeds (v. Wigan)

RUGBY UNION CLUB HONOURS

Scottish Division One Championship with Kelso – 1987–88
English Division One Championship with Newcastle – 1997–98
Sanyo Challenge with Newcastle (v. World XV) – 1997–98

INDIVIDUAL HONOURS

Twice winner of the Harry Sunderland Trophy for man of the match awarded in Premiership Rugby League final (first player to retain the trophy)

Winner: Famous Grouse Scottish Player of the Five Nations Championship – 1998

Runner-up: Famous Grouse Scottish Player of the Five Nations Championship – 1997